MY FACE IS BLACK

By C. Eric Lincoln:

THE BLACK MUSLIMS IN AMERICA
MY FACE IS BLACK

MY FACE IS
BLACK

by C. Eric Lincoln

BEACON PRESS   **BOSTON**

Copyright © 1964 by C. Eric Lincoln

Library of Congress catalogue card number: 64-22695

Published simultaneously in Canada by S. J. Reginald Saunders and Co.,
Ltd., Toronto

Printed in the United States of America

To Lucy

and to
Cecil, Joyce and Hilary

Foreword

Twenty-two million Negroes in the United States grow increasingly restive under the residuals of racial discrimination and prejudice. Their frustration increases as they see less advanced peoples assume political and social roles which they as citizens of an advanced Christian culture have yet to attain, and as they discover more and more about the white man's moral and tactical vulnerability. And there are increasing pressures from within. There is developing a radical element within the Negro sub-group which covets the leadership of the leaderless masses who have yet to commit themselves to traditional forms of Negro protest. The "critical mass" of black men and women in America has not been heard from. They do not sit-in; they do not march; they do not belong to the NAACP. They have lost faith in the ability of Negro leadership to rescue them from their misery, and they do not believe that the federal government or any other agency directed by white men is truly concerned with bringing them to a place of equality in this society. They are being pushed nearer and nearer the brink of a kind of chauvinistic anxiety, and we may well expect the symptoms of their condition to become increasingly pronounced.

The caste system in America has wittingly or unwittingly created a social Frankenstein with which we will inevitably have to deal, either at the level of love or at the level of revolution. The Negro in America, the man whose face is black, and being black is anonymous, is turning away from the American Dream and from the hope that he will be delivered by it. The dream has been progressively, and perhaps inevitably, eroded by the *mood ebony*, the willingness to be black, and the willingness to damn anyone who is not. It is the rejection of the dream and of the symbols which characterize the white man's society. It is the white man who is to be hated or ignored as the Negro has been hated and ignored for so long. It is the rejection of nonviolence as a viable method of softening the hardness of the white man's heart! It is the rejection of his religion, because that religion has been productive of paradoxes which suffering has not resolved. It is the readiness to turn to a "Man on a Black Horse" because the White Horsemen have not delivered. It is the stirring of the inarticulate masses who have grown restive with waiting and disappointment.

The warning is in the air, and in the press and on the streets. Let Responsible America take notice.

C. E. L.

Atlanta, Georgia
July, 1964

Contents

P. 81 →

CONTENTS

MY FACE IS BLACK

Chapter 1

THE AMERICAN TRAGEDY:
A Christian Dilemma

For in the beginning did not
God cast all men in a single
mould?

No man above another
But man to man a brother.[1]

The American Tragedy

My face is black. This is the central fact of my existence, the focal point of all meaning so long as I live in
America. I cannot transcend my blackness, but this is only
a personal inconvenience. The fact that America cannot
transcend it—this is the tragedy of America. The tragedy is
that a hundred years after my country (for it is my country) purged its political and social conscience of the *fact* of
human slavery as a legal institution—supported and maintained by a Christian society—it has not purged its moral
consciousness. The sentiments of slavery are now perpetu-
ated in other institutions by other names. For all our social
progress, we have maintained in our attitudes and in our
behavior persistent elements of the slave-holding mentality.
The slaves are "free," but our minds are unfree, for we did
not free the slaves as a matter of conscience but as a matter

of political convenience. So long as our minds are unfree, neither the erstwhile slaves nor their masters have been effectively emancipated.

Twenty years ago Dr. Ralph Bunche, a man who throughout his life has been doggedly persistent in his faith in his country and the inevitability of eventual justice, made a brave statement for those times. Said Dr. Bunche:

> Every man in the street, white, black, red or yellow, knows that this is the "land of the free," the "land of opportunity," the "cradle of liberty," the "home of democracy," that the American flag symbolizes the "equality of all men," and guarantees to us all the "protection of life, liberty, and property," freedom of speech, freedom of religion, and racial tolerance.[2]

Today, when we think of Little Rock and Birmingham, we know that for all the wistfulness in that brave and patriotic voice of twenty years ago, it was but a voice crying deep in the wilderness of another reality, scarcely heard and briefly noted. There is a certain poignancy about the life and personality of Dr. Bunche: a brilliant statesman, trained in our oldest university, he has given himself to his country without reservation and, more remarkably, without bitterness. In the Sophoclean sense, he is a tragic hero with one tragic flaw. He is black, and his country will never permit him to forget it. He is the victim of a peculiar institution that suffered its formal demise a hundred years ago.

During the uneasy days following the Supreme Court's 1954 decision banning segregation in the schools, an Alabama minister was asked whether he planned to urge compliance upon his congregation. "That would be preposterous," he is reported to have retorted. "My people still believe in slavery!"

Despite so candid a disclosure of the extreme attitudes of some church-goers in Alabama, slavery *is* dead. It will never again be a viable issue in this civilization. And yet the question of slavery remains pertinent to any assessment of contemporary human relations because of its pervasiveness in coloring the philosophies we adopt in seeking to come to terms (or to avoid coming to terms) with the nettlesome issues of segregation and civil rights. The slavery complex is like carrion. You have to bury it deeply or the first rainy day it will be washed up again; the first hot day you'll smell it; and the first windy day its malodorous putridness will be abroad in the whole community.

The slavery complex is like a disease. Unless you quarantine it, it will spread—first to those who are constitutionally weak, then wherever insecurity has lowered human resistance. It may also be inherited, not biologically, but as a social heritage, weakening the future generations of Americans and compromising their fitness to confront effectively the kind of a world in which they, not we, will have to live.

The slavery complex is very much like race prejudice, an unhappy phenomenon that is universal in America.

Our national tragedy is that we have been called— or we have determined—to assume international political leadership at a time when we are demonstrably unready to undertake that role with confidence or dignity. Our hands are red with the blood so recently shed in Oxford and Birmingham and Jackson, Mississippi. The tragedy is that we will shed more blood, and the knowledge of our helplessness to keep the peace at home while ensuring for every American the proper exercise of his elemental rights of citizenship presents a moral dilemma of the most serious consequence in our representation abroad. We are unprepared to deal equitably with the diverse populations of Asia and Africa because we have never dealt equitably with the diverse elements in our population at home.

An Indian visiting in Indianapolis stopped to eat in a restaurant near the YMCA where he was staying. When told that he could not be served, he replied with some sadness, "I am sorry, I have come a long way—10,000 miles." On learning that the would-be diner was not an American Negro, the manager was profuse in his apologies. But the damage had been done. Our government itself has been directly embarrassed on more than one occasion by the bigotry of restauranteurs and landlords in the Washington area, for there even the diplomats who have come here at our official invitation have not been immune to insult if they happened to be black.

Our national self-confidence is emasculated by guilt. The realization that the demands and needs of the emergent non-white nations on the other side of this shrunken world are but the counterparts of the demands and needs of our minorities at home robs us of the dynamism that is the ordinary corollary of sincere purpose and motivation. How can we talk about freedom in Angola or in South Africa when twenty-two million American *citizens* are not free! In his searching study of the contemporary racial crisis, Charles Silberman (whose status as a Jew is not altogether imprecarious) risks the wrath of bigots when he says that "the tragedy of race relations in the United States is that there is no American Dilemma, [for] white Americans are *not* torn and tortured by the conflict between their devotion to the American creed and their actual behavior. . . . What troubles them," Mr. Silberman insists, "is not that justice is being denied but that their peace is being shattered and their business interrupted."[3]

It is anomalous that we should talk about raising the standard of living in Egypt when we have not yet learned to employ people at home on the basis of merit rather than skin color! Our tragedy is the hang-dog hypocrisy with which we must go about our international affairs. We have had so little experience in honestly confronting our own problems in social relations that we have learned little that will be of benefit to us in our international responsibilities. Our major experiences have been those of apathy, evasion, tokenism and deceit. We dare to talk about the absence of democracy in Ghana—a nation but recently "emerged" from colonialism, when after almost two hundred years in the democratic experiment we can neither guarantee nor protect the right of citizens to vote! Our political stakes in Africa and Asia are crucial, but how are we to deal effectively with non-whites whose voting rights we can't suppress? Whose jobs we can't control? Whose education we can't circumscribe? And whom we can't segregate?

Our tragedy is the divisiveness which characterizes our national image. Where unity is a distressing need, we are intent upon separation. In the face of the worldwide, unrelenting challenge of the old order of racial pre-emption and racial proscription, we persist in perversity as we scramble about trying to maintain the rotted walls of segregation. It takes an army to protect the rights of one Negro in the University of his native state. As a nation we have devoted far more energy, more time and more effort to keeping Negroes out of houses, out of jobs, out of schools, out of restaurants, out of the front ends of buses and the back ends of trains, out of parks, playgrounds, night clubs and churches than we have devoted to keeping the Russians out of Cuba and out of Washington.

This is our tragedy. We are confronted with the ubiquitous specter of Communism, an insidious, implacable foe, which is avowedly dedicated to the destruction of our entire way of life. And yet we remain intent upon preserving an anachronistic facet of American democracy which needs to degrade one-tenth of the population in order that the remainder may enjoy a heightened sense of self-esteem. Indeed we seem determined that, should the Russians some day overwhelm us, they may find our cities destroyed and our people living in caves, but we will be able to present them intact our blessed system of segregation.

How frustrating it would be to our surviving population if, when we crawled out of our segregated holes in the ground to treat with the invaders, they turned out to be Chinese rather than Russian! Having spent our strength on the preservation of racial segregation at any cost, how cruel would seem our fate if our conquerors were yellow, and not white!

Our American tragedy is that we have been so obsessed with race that we have insulated ourselves from truth and reason. Our moral perspectives are frightening studies in distortion. Our social thinking and our social behavior are so seldom related to the moral principles we loudly extol in the abstract that to most of us our moral schizophrenia is a normal way of life. For example, we see no inconsistency in requiring all of our citizens to pay taxes while denying some of our citizens access to tax-supported schools and hospitals. We see no inconsistency in requiring all of our citizens to mobilize in time of war for the protection of our country, while denying some of those same citizens the protection of their homes and families once the war is over. We see no inconsistency in selling to those from whom we will not buy and to whom we will not give jobs.

Indeed, we see no inconsistency in admitting that twenty-two million people are *bona fide* American citizens and at the same time expecting them to be content with far less than citizenship implies. The critics of democracy have pointed out with telling impact that American citizenship provides few immunities for Negroes. Malcolm X has declared that "a cat can have kittens in an oven, but that doesn't make them biscuits!"[4] Similarly, being born in America is not a guarantee to any American Negro that he will enjoy the fruits of his citizenship. Malcolm X reasons that "a citizen is a person who can do whatever other citizens can do," a simple piece of logic with which it is difficult to quarrel.

In America it is generally conceded that Negroes may have the "form" of citizenship, while the "content," or most of it, is reserved for whites. But the greatest insult to the loyalties and the dignity of twenty-two million American Negroes is that the country for which they have fought and bled and died sees no inconsistency in granting to our sworn enemies (who happen to be white) the privileges, prerogatives and protection which it denies to Negroes (who happen to be black). This is the American tragedy.

John Steinbeck assesses our moral schizophrenia when he says:

> I am constantly amazed at the qualities we expect in Negroes. No race has ever offered another such high regard. We expect Negroes to be wiser than we are, braver, more dignified than we, more self-controlled and self-disciplined . . . We expect them to obey rules we flout, to be more courteous, more gallant, more proud, more steadfast. In a word, while maintaining that Negroes are inferior to us, by our unquestioning faith in them we prove our convictions that they are superior in many fields, even fields we are presumed to be trained and conditioned in and they are not.[5]

But the greatest tragedy of all is the growing disillusionment, the sense of dereliction and despair—the creeping suspicion in the hearts of more and more Negroes in America that neither law nor longing, nor love, nor loyalty is going to bring them any time soon to that place of freedom for which their fathers sighed; for which their children cry. The tragedy is that although we have come far, we have not come far enough. That although society has relented a little here and a little there, it has done so grudgingly and in extremely bad grace. We have failed to recognize the compulsive concern for human dignity which has energized the civilized world in recent years, and we have made great issues of picayune matters which prudent men could have resolved with the stroke of a pen or the removal of a sign. In the mid-twentieth century how important is it to maintain "white" and "colored" signs over identical fountains in the Sears and Roebuck store? In a civilized society, how crucial is it to prohibit the same kids who go unmolested to a record shop to buy a record from going to the municipal library to check out a book? Segregation is not only demeaning. It is also inconvenient.

In the post-war era, when America became busily engaged in the reconstruction of a brave new world overseas, had we given our attention seriously and in good faith to the ordering of our own society to the end that all Americans might be at least as free as those whose freedom we were championing abroad, there would have been no Little Rock, no New Orleans, no Oxford, Mississippi. We would not have reaped the harvest of ridicule and condemnation we did reap from the capitals of the world and we would not have loosed the resentment and the hatred, the suspicion and the fear which continue to poison the relations between black and white Americans of this generation.

The Negro in America suspects that the white man still thinks in terms of a "place" for him. And this is the crux of the matter: does he, or does he not? We now know that caste has no place in a modern democracy, and the Negro has repudiated the imputation of a special place for him at any level, in any aspect of social behavior. The tragedy is that he waited so long to make this determination, for in deciding finally to be *wholly* free within the meaning of democratic freedom, the Negro has helped America to confront its own conscience and to learn the truth about itself. As a contemporary clergyman has said, "The world is now too dangerous for anything but truth, too small for anything but brotherhood."[6] Brotherhood *is* truth. And there is neither truth nor beauty in human relations in the absence of brotherhood. The tragedy is that the most obvious and simple truths are sometimes the most difficult to learn.

It is easy to convince oneself that America is not interested in knowing the truth. James Baldwin asserts that
"the crime of which I accuse my country and my countrymen . . . [is] that they have destroyed and are destroying
hundreds of thousands of lives and do not know it and do
not want to know it." It is this studied obliviousness against
which today's black youth rebels. They are determined that
the white man shall not escape culpability by the simple
technique of refusing to recognize that a crime against them
has occurred and is occurring. "This innocent country,"
writes Baldwin in an imaginary letter to Negro youth, "set
you down in a ghetto in which, in fact, it intended that you
should perish . . . You were born where you were born and
faced the future that you faced because you were black and
for no other reason."[7]

The tragedy is that America has ignored its better conscience, even from the beginning, and wherever the still,
small voice has tried to make itself heard, it has been
drowned out in the shrill demogoguery of hatred and bigotry. In one of the first drafts of the Declaration of Independence Thomas Jefferson sought to arraign the English
king for his "cruel war against human nature itself, violating
its most sacred rights of life and liberty in the persons of a
distant people who never offended him, captivating and
carrying them into slavery in another hemisphere, or to in-
cur miserable death in their transportation thither." But the
objections of the delegates from Georgia and South Carolina prevailed and all reference to slavery was deleted from
that basic document of American freedom.

One wonders whether it would have made any difference in the shaping of American history had that indictment

against human bondage been preserved. Jefferson, himself a slaveholder, confessed to his countrymen that "I tremble for my country when I reflect that God is just, and his justice cannot sleep forever." And in a startling moment of clairvoyance George Washington was later to reveal his own misgivings about the immorality and the danger of the Negro's thralldom. Of the Negroes he said, "I shall be very happily mistaken if they are not found to be a very troublesome species of property ere many years have passed over our heads." That "troublesome species of property" first traded at Jamestown 350 years or so ago is still with the American conscience, I fear. And there seems to be little reason to believe that the trouble will abate until the concept of property—the arrogant notion that the Negro is a thing, a brute, a nonentity—has been eradicated from the innermost recesses of the white man's mind, and the more reasonable concept that he is a free and equal person has been established in its place.[8]

The Christian Dilemma

About 1830, a free Negro whose name was David Walker dared to call into question the religious pretensions of the American white man. Demanded Walker in his *Appeal in Four Articles:*

> Can anything be a greater mockery of religion than the way it is conducted by the Americans? It appears as though they are bent only on daring Almighty God to do his best . . . They drive us around the country like brutes and go into the house of the God of Justice to return thanks for having aided them in their infernal cruelties inflicted upon us.[9]

In his recent book, *Black Religion*,[10] Dr. Joseph R.
Washington, Jr., Chaplain at Dickinson College in Pennsyl-
vania, asserts that "the record of the dominant religious
forces in America is clear—'No Negroes Allowed,' or to put
it in the affirmative, 'For Whites Only.' The real story of the
American Negro," Dr. Washington says, "is his exclusion
from the currents of mainstream Protestantism and Roman
Catholicism." Racial segregation at any level is evil. As public policy in our national life it has brought us weakness and
turmoil at home and ridicule and embarrassment abroad.
This is what segregation in its secular expression has meant
to America. In the church its presence is morally corrosive
and it presents a dilemma for every Christian who loves both
God and the church (which is the confraternity of the
godly).

A recent issue of the race relations publication of the
Secretariat on Racial and Ethnic Relations of the World
Council of Churches tells how the British people have found
themselves in an unhappy dilemma because of the conflict
between their religious teachings and their social behavior.
The British, who for several hundred years sent their mer-
chantmen and missionaries to almost every accessible human
habitation on earth, did not reckon on the day when their
vari-colored converts would come home to England from
the many distant lands which were once the Grand Colonial
Empire, and which now constitute the British Commonwealth. That Anglo-Saxon island now finds itself with a sizeable non-white population—Pakinstanis, Indians, West Indians, Chinese, Africans, and others. Great Britain's dilemma
is that although her historic wealth and power derived from

her colonial enterprises, and even now her economic and political survival depends in large measure upon the status of unity and reciprocity of the Commonwealth nations, the English people do not want non-white immigrants to settle in Britain. With great embarrassment the government has hastily enacted an immigration and deportation act directed at the colored immigrants to the mother country.

Furthermore, although the British missionaries brought hundreds of thousands of Africans and Asians to Christ in their native countries, these non-white Christians are not welcome in the churches of London, Sheffield, Oxford and Manchester. The question now being debated in British Christendom is whether it would not be better after all to establish "special congregations" for the non-white Christians.

The British, as you see, have reached the depths in Christian relations we plumbed a hundred years ago. They are teetering on the brink of an abyss from which we are still struggling to extricate ourselves. (Or we are at least going through the motions.) May God preserve them from so futile and so unchristian an evasion of the commandment to love! There are enough segregated Christians in the world, and over twenty million of them are stamped "made in America."

The British dilemma is the counterpart of the Christian dilemma in America, except for our relative positions on the cycle that moves from immigration to restriction, to segregation, to hyphenation. A "hypenated" Christian is one whose racial or ethnic designation is bracketed to his religion with a hyphen, making it plain that his is not *the* Christian

communion, and implying, inadvertently or not, some quali-
fication of his faith and worth. A hyphenated American is
made the same way.

We have a long history of hyphenation in America.
About the turn of the century, one of the popular sociological fantasies of the day was that America was a great
"melting pot" in which elements of the world's diverse racial
and ethnic groups were refined and fused into a new and
dramatic entity: *The American.* America was the "Mother
of Exiles," who bade the world

> "Keep ancient lands your stories pomp, . . ."
> Give me your tired, your poor,
> Your huddled masses yearning to breathe free,
> The wretched refuse of your teeming shore.
> Send these, the homeless, tempest-tost, to me . . .[11]

They came: the Irish, the Poles, the Slavs, the Italians, the
Jews and others. The Indians were already here; the first
Negro came in 1492. He was Pedro Alonzo Nino, captain
of the ship on which Columbus sailed.[12] The Orientals came
too, but they were soon to be excluded,[13] for their color was
a bar to assimilation. And so, involuntarily, they joined another group of hyphenated Americans, whose color also
made them "unassimilable." The melting-pot hypothesis was
a brave illusion, but it *was* an illusion, for even when the
floodgates of immigration were most widely ajar, a significant segment of "old settlers" had never exposed their pre-
emptions to the melting-pot thinking, and the politicians and
sociologists alike soon came to know it. William Brink and
Louis Harris, in their book *The Negro Revolution in America*, report with compelling candor that "in a land noted as a

melting-pot for many cultures, the Negro has not . . . been allowed to melt." Too true. But if heat is a factor the pot in which the melting has been done seems destined to boil at some unaccustomed temperatures for a long time to come.

By the end of World War I, the melting-pot idea had been abandoned by most Americans. Assimilation had come to mean the sociological integration of individuals possessing a common *racial* identity. To all others, the gates were closed and barred.[14] When the great wave of immigration came to an end, there were millions of "hyphenated" Americans: German-Americans, Swedish-Americans, Irish-Americans, and the like. There were also Japanese-Americans, Mexican-Americans, Negro-Americans, Indian-Americans, and so forth. For some, the non-whites, the hyphenated status bids for perpetuity.

The big disappointment is that the church has been so ineffective in dealing with racial problems. Hyphenation is caste-making. "Caste" is a secular institution. It has no place in a democracy, and no sanction in the Judeo-Christian tradition. If race is a bar to social assimilation, this is a reflection of the value-constructs of our secular society or, at the very least, it reflects the moral incapacity of society to approximate its ideals. But then, we are taught that it is precisely through the instrumentality of the church that God transforms society and empowers it to lift itself above its failings. A serious problem arises, however, when the church mistakes the voice of the secular society for the voice of God. A generation ago the "social gospel" theologian Walter Rauschenbusch was alarmed at the direction in which organized religion seemed to be moving, and he issued a timely warning:

The power of religion is almost illimitable, but it is not necessarily beneficent. Religion intensifies whatever it touches, be it good or evil . . . There is no love so tender, no compassion so self-sacrificing, no courage so inspired by religion. But neither is any hatred so implacable, or any cruelty so determined as religious hatred and cruelty . . .

If the American churches cover the existing order with the shield of their protection and call on their people in the name of God and religion to keep things as they are, they will make of the short march from Egypt to the Promised Land a weary forty years' pilgrimage in the desert of Sinai. It will take incomparably longer to get results, and the results will be less complete and less stable after they are obtained.

On the other hand, if our churches take the side of the people and back the demands for social justice and fraternity in the name of Christ and the Gospel, the whole situation is changed.[15]

The church is and ought to be a conserver of values, but it is charged with a judicious discrimination as to what values it shall properly conserve. It is the task of the church to criticize and to correct the values of the society, not to sanctify them, for insofar as the church is the body of Christ, its values do not derive from the secular, nor can the church in its proper expression of the Divine Will be held accountable to any earthly power. We must obey God rather than man. The church has too often lost sight of the true nature of its high calling. Too often it has "paid its vows and decked its bed" and gone a-whoring after the approval of the ungodly. On the racial issue, the church in America has been piddling where it should have been persistent; it has been petulant where puissance might have been expected. In trying to run with the hare and hunt with the hounds the church has a confused role in the minds of its membership, for the church itself behaves very much like its secular counterparts. It finds some Christians "unassimilable," and it relegates them to perpetual hyphenation.

Negroes have borne their enforced isolation from the mainstream of Christianity with unparalleled equanimity. While they have never accepted the white man's rationalizations at face value, they have until quite recently left him to wrestle with his own conscience in the rarefied hallowedness of his segregated sanctuaries. The main thrust of the Negro's offensive for freedom and dignity has been in other directions. Indeed, many Negroes felt that once the law had spoken in clear and unmistakable terms, the white man's church would rise to help them in the implementation of the law. This it has shown no serious inclination to do. To the contrary, the supreme irony is illustrated in the fact that on occasion the church or its representatives has felt constrained to warn the Negro that in the pursuit of his constitutional rights he is proceeding incautiously and in a manner generally calculated to lose friends among white people.

Languishing in the comfortless filth of the infamous "Big Rock" jail in the equally infamous city of Birmingham, Martin Luther King, Jr., was chided by an interfaith cabal of white Alabama clergymen for leading the "unwise and untimely" protest against discrimination in that most segregated of Southern cities. In a long and impassioned epistle which subsequently claimed its place in the history of the civil rights struggle as "A Letter from Birmingham Jail," King reminded his critics of the moral insignificance of the churches they represent. "I have watched white churches stand on the sidelines and merely mouth pious irrelevancies and sanctimonious trivialities. Over and over again I have found myself asking: 'What kind of people worship here? Who is their God?' "[16]

How often have Negroes pondered these questions over the centuries of their bondage! How insensate has been the church never to have known (or possibly never to have cared) that from the earliest days of slavery when the mealy-mouthed preachers brought the Pauline doctrine of "servants, obey your masters!" to the compounds around the slave quarters, the slaves *knew*! They knew *then* the collusion of the church with the institution dedicated to their dehumanization, and, knowing, they rejected the white man's church and the white man's spurious doctrine. Hiding in the woods and the swamps, they sang the songs of faith and deliverance ("Oh didn't my Lord deliver Daniel!") and, when they were finally free, they organized their own churches.

The Catholic, Jewish and Protestant clergymen who resolved their own differences long enough to cast a collective stone at Dr. King could have accomplished more for the faiths they represent, their respective congregations and the good of their own souls had they themselves gone to jail. One is reminded of Henry David Thoreau who, on having been arrested for civil disobedience, was allegedly asked by Ralph Waldo Emerson, an astonished (but proper) Bostonian: "Henry, what are you doing in there?" "A better question," said Thoreau, "is Waldo, what are you doing out there?"

As the Christian church was the tool of slavery, so has it been a bastion of segregation. As other barriers crumble before the relentless march of federal law and economic expediency, the church is trapped by its own inconsistencies. As a moral agent the church is fully aware that it should lead in healing the broken community—in establishing the principle of brotherhood in its own congregations and wherever else its influence is respected. As a conservator of values, it has put an inordinate valuation on racial exclusiveness and, since it is essentially immune to both law and economic expediency, it bids fair to be among the last institutions to desegregate. Traditionally, the church has sought to escape its dilemma by making noble pronouncements about love and brotherhood at the level of national policy without expecting much to happen at the level of local action.

At the 1964 General Assembly of the Southern Presbyterian Church, Rosco Nix, a Negro layman from Washington, D. C., articulated his own frustrations and those of Negro Christians everywhere when he blurted out in an emotion-laden voice: "Will the Church be the last fortress of segregation?"[17] The answer, brother Nix, is most likely, "Yes!" Mr. Nix startled no one when he charged that today's youth of whatever race "looks to secular institutions for moral truths rather than to the Church." The church has apparently accepted this as a price it must pay for its forfeiture of leadership in human relations. Our children are demonstrably unimpressed by proscriptions against smoking and drinking and sexual license when they see with their own eyes the fruits of the inhumanity of their fathers.

Obviously, there must be no segregation anywhere in the church. There is something spiritually profane and morally obscene in the separation of Christians in the church. Being a Christian, like being a "person," implies community. No individual existence is a "person" in isolation from others

of its kind.[18] To deny a human being the human associations
and the opportunities to share in the human experiences that
make of a "being" a "person" would be tragic beyond expression. How much more tragic it is to deny Christians un-
restricted fellowship in the church! Segregation is by its very
nature a bar to meaningful Christian fellowship, for it creates
distinctions where no distinctions can morally exist. Surely
race is transcended wherever true Christians meet.

The dilemma of segregation has a double edge, for no
believer can fully experience the richness of the faith except
as one angle of an Eternal Triangle with God and his fellow
man. The essential values of true religion, like the complete
fulfillment of personality, are qualified severely by the unwillingness to know and to enter into dynamic relationship
with others. In the Eternal Triangle, every man who loves
God seeks to know and to love God's "other image," whatever that "other image" may be. Every Christian shares with
every other Christian the image of God, and is thereby to
some degree reflective of the personality of God. Our crisis
seems to derive from an idolatrous confusion of God with
man. Christianity in America is preoccupied not with how
nearly fellow Christians reflect the personality of God, but
rather with how nearly they approximate the current racial
ideal. In short, we have borrowed the bigoted values of the
secular world and superimposed them upon the eternal uni-
versals of the faith!

The Negro Christian is confronted with a double alienation. He suffers the universal estrangement of human finitude that separates him from God; and as if this ultimate
isolation were not enough, he must also bear the artificial
and unrealistic estrangement of racial prejudice that sepa-

rates him from his brothers in Christ (and out)! This human
estrangement is unnatural. It is productive of an extreme
level of discreative anxiety, for it can neither be rationalized
nor overcome by any capacities available to its victims. Here
is a paradox. Demanding nothing, the forgiving love of God
reaches out and bridges the chasm of spiritual alienation, and
the knowledge of this love is inspiring and reassuring. But
human fellowship demands an impossible premium: it is not
enough that a man be made in the image of God; he must be
cookie-cut after a racial ideal which is, in fact, a delusion.
Arnold Toynbee speaks directly to the problem when he
says:

> How different [was the medieval Western Christian] from
> the spirit in which the white-skinned Western Protestant
> of modern times regards his black-skinned convert. The
> convert may have found spiritual salvation in the White
> Man's faith; he may have acquired the White Man's culture
> and learnt to speak his language with the tongue of an angel;
> he may have become adept in the White Man's economic
> technique, and yet it profits him nothing so long as he has
> not changed his skin. Surely he can retort that it profits the
> White Man nothing to understand all mysteries and all
> knowledge and have skill so that he can move mountains,
> so long as he has not charity.[19]

The unity of the church and the integrity of its pre-
cepts presupposes a common faith, a common Father, a common fate and a common community at the level of worship
and fellowship. This *must* be so if the life and the teachings
of Jesus are in any way pertinent to the Christian faith in its
day-to-day expression. As Christians, we have been long on
pronouncements and embarrassingly short on performance.

Dr. Thomas Pettigrew, writing in *The Christian Century*, observes that "at the higher levels, every major Christian denomination has made it clear that racial integration is a Christian imperative. At the lower levels, omitting some outstanding exceptions, the Church offers little but discriminatory practices and segregated establishments."[20]

Negroes do not want to be hyphenated Christians. They do not want to be segregated Americans. They do not want to be a part of any enterprise, any institution, any collective endeavor which stigmatizes them or compromises their sense of worth as persons. The churches have often been charitable, but without charity. There comes a time when human dignity requests and self-respect demands that we cease doing things *for* people and do things *with* people.

It is the shame of democratic Christian America that across the country twenty million black Christians have put 180 million white Christians to flight. As the Negro has migrated to the cities in search of a fairer share of the common values of this society, the white Christians have seldom stayed to be neighborly. Abandoning their homes and their churches, their schools and their playgrounds, their consciences and sometimes their faith, they have fled to the suburbs where no Negroes are, *yet*. The Negroes who move in where the whites have moved out observe bitterly that only the white man's businesses are left to welcome them.

Despite their skepticism about Christian motivation in the white churches in general, many Negroes and many white Christians of deep devotional commitment maintain hope that the church will yet purge itself. The Rev. Benjamin Mays, president of Morehouse College and an internationally known leader in religious and educational circles, laments poignantly the failure of the church to accept real responsibility in the troublesome area of race relations. Writing in *The Christian Century*, Dr. Mays confesses:

> Admittedly the churches have not led, but certainly they should have followed. How unfortunate it is that immediately after May 17, 1954 [the date of the Supreme Court decision ending segregation in the schools], our local religious leaders did not assume moral leadership, did not take a courageous stand and work for implementation of the Supreme Court's decision . . . How wonderful it would have been if our religious leaders had pointed out the moral and religious bases of that decision, [and] had led their people to accept the decision not merely because they believe in law and order but primarily because they recognize that prejudice, segregation and discrimination based on race and culture are sinful, immoral and contrary to the religious principles which Sunday after Sunday are proclaimed from our pulpits.[21]

In spite of his bitter disappointment in the institution, which for him and for millions of other Negroes and whites is the key to a more humane civilization, Dr. Mays' conviction in the inevitable moral triumph of the church is not shaken. "The churches will follow," he asserts bravely at the conclusion of his lament. Doubtless he is correct: the churches will follow, but not in time to avoid the consequences of their recalcitrance. Generations will pass before the confidence of the people will be restored, and ere the deep wound that segregation has dealt the body of Christ will be healed.

The low state of affairs in the Christian churches may not be laid exclusively at the door of the white man, for the

quality of the Negro's religion, like that of his white con-
temporaries, has suffered some serious spiritual erosion. The
Negro's religion is too often too superficial, too ego-
centered, too pragmatic and too reflective of the exigencies
of the social milieu against which it must be lived and prac-
ticed. A religion which is truly vital must transcend as well
as transform a society which is inimical to its values. Our
present dilemma is that our society is in such dire need of
transformation that we have lost sight of the relevance of the
transcendent quality of religion at its best. White people do
not seem to realize that whatever the Negro's failings or
shortcomings may be, they are subject to refinement in the
presence of the spirit of Christ. Certainly, if this is not true,
then preaching is vain; but equally vain are the pragmatic
arrangements of fearful and faithless men. Ultimately they
will not prevail.

Negroes do not seem to know that the abandonment of
their historic faith in God and their trust that man may be
somehow brought about to do the will of God has not contributed favorably to their cause, however just that cause
may be. That they have been disillusioned by the posture of
the church in the matter of social justice is not sufficient
reason to abandon it as a meaningful force in the quality of
all civilization. Dr. Pettigrew predicts that unless the church
moves rapidly to implement its ideals at the parish level,
"organized Protestantism will have become largely a fraternal order, [and] will no longer be an effective moral force
in our society." Too many Negroes have prematurely
reached the conclusion that the church has already become
just that: a fraternal order with designated chapters for
whites and others restricted to Negroes in keeping with the

traditional arrangements of the social order. Seen as a social rather than as a spiritual institution, it is less difficult and less painful to reconcile the behavior of the church with the principles it has professed, for moral schizophrenia is the norm of the secular world in America.

Seen from any other perspective, the right of Christians to worship and fellowship together, and the expectation that they will, is so elemental in terms of the implications of the Christian faith that a segregated church would seem to be preposterous. Consciously or unconsciously, the Negroes in the church have been brought to the position that if the church cannot be a fellowship of Christians alike in mind and spirit, however different the color of their skins or the shape of their noses, then the churches as social organizations may as well be utilized in the all-out battle for human dignity.

To the mind of the Negro the segregated church is the rawest symbol of the white man's inability to practice the Christianity he has sought to sell to millions of non-whites around the world. Sometimes the Negro remembers with bitterness how as a slave he accepted the white man's spiritual teachings, only to find that when he became a citizen the teachings did not apply. It is difficult to forget that in order to be a Christian in America the Negro has been required either to organize new churches or denominations, or accept an uncomplimentary status in white churches where his presence is not desired.

How can we wonder at the thousands who join the cults of Daddy Grace and Father Divine? How can Christian America be surprised that Elijah Muhammad has attracted tens of thousands of Negroes to the cause of Black Islam? Considering the fact that for approximately three hundred years Christianity was the American Negro's only religious option, we may well believe that, had the Christian church been able to overcome its racial bias, the Negro's long tradition in that church would have remained unbroken.

In 1787 a group of Negro Methodists withdrew from the Methodist Episcopal church in Philadelphia. The critical issue was segregation. These Christians who believed Christianity and segregation to be logical contradictions went on to found the African Methodist Episcopal Church, with a current membership of more than 1,200,000—the second largest Methodist body in America.

In 1796, Negro members withdrew from the John Street Church in New York City. Again the issue was segregation. Today the church born of that protest—the African Methodist Episcopal Zion Church, remains a separate spiritual entity with a membership of approximately one million.

In 1867 the Virginia Baptist State Convention was formed of churches organized to escape segregation in the Baptist churches. Today there are 7,000,000 Negroes in three Baptist Conventions.

In the Presbyterian Church, Negro membership dropped from 31,000 in 1861 to 1,300 in 1916. The issue was segregation. I could go on, but the point, I think, is established.

The contemporary Negro is in many ways a tragic figure—jealous of his freedom and his dignity, hunting, hunting a church where he can worship God in the absence of bigotry.

Roman Catholicism has claimed many in recent years. At the turn of the century, less than 1 percent of the Negro Christians belonged to the Catholic communion, and at the

time of World War I, 90 percent of all Negro Christians
were either Methodists or Baptists. Even as late as the 1930's,
there was a current saying that if a Negro were not Methodist or Baptist, someone had been tampering with his religion. Times have changed. The Negro's search is no longer
for a place to worship, but for a place in which he can worship in dignity. He is willing to experiment—far from the
familiar shores of the Methodist and Baptist churches—white
or black. The Unitarians have begun to attract the Negro
intellectuals, not in large numbers, but a few. The number
of Negroes in Roman Catholic churches is steadily increasing. Even Bahai and the various Hindu sects have a sprin-
kling of Negro members in the larger cities.

The increasing repugnance of traditional Christianity
to the Negro's aspirations for freedom and dignity is not
limited to America. All over Africa Christianity is against
the wall. The Rev. Billy Graham reported after his visit
there that for every African choosing Christianity, ten are
now choosing Islam. Why? Because in true Islam there is no
color line. The churches of America have probably been
rendered a gratuitous service by the distorted picture of
Islam presented by the Black Muslim Movement. At a time
when any separatist philosophy is repugnant to the Negro's
concept of social and religious propriety, Elijah Muhammad
has managed to wean untold thousands of Negroes (including a sizeable number of former Christian pastors) away
from the churches and weld them into a white-despising
black supremacy cult called the Black Muslim Movement.

If his options are viable, the rank-and-file American
Negro wants neither black supremacy nor white supremacy
—so he is somewhat appalled at the Black Muslim philosophy

and has hesitated to identify with it in really significant numbers. As a result, at a time when Christianity is in serious default, the spread of orthodox Islam among American Negroes is certainly inhibited in this country because it has been erroneously identified with the racist doctrines of Elijah Muhammad, who teaches his followers that the white man is an incarnation of the devil; that Christianity is his historic strategy for the pacification and the perpetual enslavement of all who are not white; and that the Negro preacher is the white man's most effective agent for corralling his black brethren and narcotizing them with the venomous poisons of the white man's religion. Malcolm X, as we shall see, intends to remedy that situation by introducing large numbers of his admirers to a more orthodox rendition of traditional Islam.

Christianity (the Black Muslims and the white segregationists to the contrary) is not a white man's religion. It is a religion for all mankind, and its fundamental social expressions are love and brotherhood. In the absence of these there can be no Christian religion.

The Christian world is now confronted with a complex of challenges that are unprecedented in Christian history: how shall we conquer the cancer of atheistic communism which continues to infect the have-not nations of the world? Surely we know by now that what they "have not" cannot be supplied satisfactorily by more shoes, tools and bread!

What is to be our answer to the bitter nationalism of the newly emergent nations, which have so often tended to throw out the baby of Christianity with the bath of colonialism?

Have we a convincing answer to the resurgence of an

aggressive Islam—preaching brotherhood and meaning it? Arnold Toynbee reminds us that ". . . white Muslims . . . have always been free from color prejudice *vis-à-vis* the non-white races. . . . They divide mankind into Believers and Unbelievers who are potentially Believers; and this division cuts across every difference of physical race."

What is our posture before the awesome specter of a common annihilation in some nuclear holocaust? Shall we have hyphenated worship in segregated holes in the ground? Have we perfected a program to

> People the planets in outer space
> Sect by sect, and race by race . . . ?

Finally, what of the Negroes who were driven from the churches by bigotry a hundred years ago, and who are still kept out, or given hyphenated status, or "annexed" by one specious means or another by today's big denominations? What Christian commitments are the church, *and the people in the churches*, willing to make *now* to bridge the chasm between all those who would be brothers in Christ? The positions taken at the 1964 national meetings of the Presbyterian Church and the Methodist Church to integrate their synods and jurisdictions by 1967 and 1968, respectively, is encouraging, but this action is long overdue. Even at this late date it is opposed by a vociferous minority of white Christians in both churches.

If you are to understand the meaning of Malcolm X, you must first understand that American Negroes are *tired* of the white man's chicanery; tired of the white man's curious religion; tired of moving back; tired of "going around"; tired of waiting. Rosa Parks was a symbol of the

Negro's weariness. Malcolm X is a symbol of the recklessness that extreme weariness can produce. Religion could
have played—perhaps could play still—an important part in
alleviating the weariness and forestalling the recklessness
that may plunge this society into bloodshed.

No, Christianity is not a white man's religion, but if
bigotry is not unseated in the churches and in the society at
large, Christianity may well be left to the white man. And
welcome. There is no mood today, anywhere in the world,
to compromise human dignity in the interest of maintaining
an anachronistic system of social relations based on such
arbitrary values as the color of one's skin. Gordon W. All-
port, Harvard University's eminent social psychologist,
warns us that

> The day of reckoning has come for the Christian Church.
> The world is now too small, too crowded, too perilous and
> too rapidly changing to permit further temporizing with
> bigotry and discrimination . . . The task is difficult; the chal-
> lenge is immediate.[22]

We do not need any more "pronouncements" from
above. We do not need any more studies from below. We
do need to act. As Edmund Burke once said, "The only
thing necessary for the triumph of evil is for good men to
do nothing." The challenge is to America. What is America
going to do about it?

Chapter 2

THE FIGHT FOR FREEDOM:
Protest and Communication

> I am the son of America
> (but America has denied me)
> I am a free citizen
> (but I am denied civil privileges)
> I am a man
> (but my face is black . . .)[1]

One balmy afternoon in the late summer of 1619, a ship of the Royal Dutch Navy put about and tacked slowly into the harbor at Jamestown, Virginia. There was something about the appearance and movement of the ship—something grotesque and foreboding. Yes, there was something evil and repulsive about the way she stood silently off-shore as if surveying the brave new land before bringing it a cargo of doom. An unaccustomed shudder of apprehension shook the little body of colonists waiting at the dockside as with an ominous rumble the long anchor chain uncoiled itself and brought the ship up fast against the wharf.

The captain of the Dutch ship caused the plank to be lowered and went ashore, followed by as motley a crew of sailors as had ever put to sea. Their provisions were gone; their water was gone. They had no money, but the captain explained that his ship carried a cargo well worth the provisions he wanted the settlers to exchange for it. It was a strange cargo. It was a cargo of men.

Lying in the darkness in the hold of the Dutch man-o-war were one hundred separate items of human flesh chained ankle to ankle, wrist to wrist, neck to neck.

Braving the terrible stench and ignoring the cries of the suffering captives, by the dim light of the ship's lantern the Virginians picked out twenty "Negras" and carried them ashore in chains. By that act they founded in America "that most peculiar institution" which for all time since has qualified this civilization and mocked its democratic pretensions.

It was not the initial intention of the Virginia colonists to traduce their noble experiment with human slavery. The Negroes obtained from the Dutch adventurers were at first treated like any other indentured servants. But in seventeenth century Virginia labor was in short supply. The system of European indenture was troublesome and uncertain. The mortality rate among Indians forced to labor was extremely high, and when they did not die of captivity, they escaped readily into the surrounding forests.

But it was soon discovered that the supply of Negroes was inexhaustible, and there were no troublesome moral or political questions to prevent their exploitation. Since they were not Christians, they had no immunities in law or custom. Since they were not Europeans, there were no questions of international diplomacy involved. And, since they were not white, they were somehow *different* and therefore *created* for the convenience of men who *were* white, Christian and European.

The Negroes were strong and physically fit, having survived the unbelievable horrors of the "middle passage" from

Africa. They were highly visible, making escape by anonymity (a persistent problem with white bond-servants)
virtually impossible. A new world deserved a new civilization. By the middle of the sevententh century the Negro had
been unanimously elected to provide the perpetual labor
supply upon which that civilization was to be projected. He
had become a commodity, a thing to be bought and sold and
traded in the interests of a new world a-building in which
he had no interests which were recognized at law, and from
which after 250 years of toil he was to derive no compen-
sation whatever. He was destined to become a symbol of the
wealth and power of a nation, and of the debasement of the
spirit of its people. But in his own mind he was also pre-
destined to freedom in this new land, and to that end he
directed his energies from the day of his enslavement.[2]

One of the little ironies of American history is that the
Negro has always been as ready to fight for the white man's
freedom as for his own. This readiness stems in part from
the fact that from the earliest times the Negro correctly
identified his freedom with that of his country. Being free
meant being free in America. Although for the greater part
of the history of America the Negro has been in bondage to
Americans, he has until recent times been firm in his patience
and persistent in his belief that the white man would grant
him justice. He fought for American independence because
he believed that when America was free, America would
grant him freedom. He fought to "make the world safe for
democracy" because he hoped that in securing democracy
abroad, he would make democracy universal at home. He
fought for the "Four Freedoms" with full faith that they
meant freedom for everybody, including himself. Never has

he been rewarded with the fulfillment of his aspirations. While nearly every nation under the sun has enjoyed directly or indirectly the fruits of his labor and the purchase of his blood, the American Negro has had to wait, and waiting has been a long, long time.

On the second of October, 1750, there appeared in the *Boston Gazette* the following notice:

> Ran away from his master WILLIAM BROWN . . . on the 30th of September last, a [Negro] Fellow, about 27 years of age, named CRISPUS, 6 feet 2 inches high, short curl'd Hair, his Knees nearer together than common; had on a light colour'd Bear-skin Coat, plain brown Fustain Jacket, or brown All-wool one, new Buckskin Breeches, blue Yarn Stockings, and a checked woolen shirt.

> "Whoever shall take up said Runnaway, and convey him to his above-said Master, shall have ten-Pounds . . . Reward."[3]

History does not record whether the tall, knock-kneed Negro was ever "taken up" and returned to his master, but history has recorded for all time the story of his martyrdom in the cause of American freedom, for on the morning of March 5, 1770, Crispus Attucks gave his life for a freedom that he himself could only know vicariously. On that cold blustery morning a company of British soldiers marched briskly up King Street—the principal street of what was then the principal city in America. In this calculated show of force the objective was to remind the Americans of their unfreedom—their continued subjection to the British Crown, and to suppress with force any protestations of injustice or any complaints about second-class citizenship. The inference of second-class citizenship was extremely distasteful to the Americans then, even as it is to Americans now. They were taxed without having a voice in the government which taxed them, and their economic and personal behavior was restricted by impersonal forces which had no knowledge and less concern for them as individuals with the normal human desires for identity and respect. Taxation without representation is tyranny; no self-respecting citizenry will long accept responsibility where common privilege is unreasonably withheld or too long deferred.

So it was that when the British soldiers swung arrogantly up the street—resplendent in their scarlet uniforms and confident in the superiority of their arms and in their self-conceived "inherent" superiority as Englishmen and Anglo-Saxons, they ought not to have been surprised to find themselves challenged. Men who have been long oppressed are not impressed by superior arms in the hands of either tyrants or bigots who are committed to force and intimidation rather than the honest negotiation of grievances. Men who have caught a glimpse of freedom do not pale before the conceit of a presumptive arrogance of race, class or nationality.

Facing the British at the end of King Street (now called State Street), was a handful of patriots. At their head was Crispus Attucks, a black man who had established his personal freedom by running away as a youth, but who now as a man had returned to play his part in making available a more complete freedom to every American—including the white man who had put a price on his head. As the company of redcoats approached, Attucks turned to his motley group of followers: "The way to get rid of these soldiers," he shouted, "is to attack . . . !"

With sticks and clubs and pitchforks and whatever weapons came to hand, the Americans did attack, Crispus Attucks at their head. The British soldiers opened fire and the escaped slave was the first to fall. Three men died with Attucks at the Boston Massacre, but the struggle against tyranny had been joined decisively, and ultimately the cause of freedom and justice would prevail. For some, but not for all. It is for the others that the fight continues in the streets of America today. Today all Americans are indeed free, but we are not yet *equally* free. We have been a long time completing the job begun in Boston so many years ago.

Thousands of Negroes, free men and slaves fought in the revolutionary armies. Many distinguished themselves: Peter Salem at Bunker Hill; Lemuel Haynes at Ticonderoga. Prince Whipple and Oliver Cromwell were with Washington at the historic crossing of the Delaware. There was Deborah Garnett, a Negro woman whose love of country was so strong that she disguised herself as a man in order to serve with the Continental Army. Upon being discharged she was cited for "extraordinary heroism." Negroes fought at Lexington, Concord, White Plains, Trenton, Saratoga, Savannah and a hundred other places in the cause of freedom. Of all the colonies, only South Carolina and Georgia persisted in opposing their enlistment. They were to fight again in the War of 1812, where at the Battle of New Orleans they contributed significantly to Andrew Jackson's victory, and in the Spanish-American War, where at San Juan Hill they saved the "Rough Riders" of Theodore Roosevelt from extermination. And in two World Wars, in faraway places all over the earth, they have responded to freedom's cry for help.

But freedom is as elusive as it is treasured. It has been the tradition in America that once the white man has control of it he has been loath to share it unrestrictedly with anybody else. As a consequence the Negro has been placed in the paradoxical position of fighting for a common freedom and then fighting for his share. Indeed, the history of the black man in America is the history of one long fight to be free. Contrary to the popular fiction of the Negro's docile acceptance of slavery, there were more than one hundred *recorded* slave revolts in America between 1663 and 1884.[4] In addition there were no fewer than fifty-five revolts at sea. Since it was the practice to suppress vigorously all news about slave uprisings (lest they become infectious), it is reasonable to assume that scores of insurrections must have gone unreported, while others await the laborious searching out of the historian.

At least four major uprisings deserve the attention of anyone interested in trying to assess the depth of the revolutionary spirit energizing today's Negro revolt. In the spring of 1800, a young Negro named Gabriel Prosser began laying plans to sack Richmond and take the state of Virginia. By August his plans were complete, and some two thousand Negroes had been enrolled in his underground movement. At midnight on August 30, one thousand of the revolutionaries met outside the sleeping city of Richmond armed with homemade swords, pikes and guns stolen from the plantations. The company was divided into four task forces. One was to seize the arsenal and a second the powder house, while the two remaining units would march on the city from opposite ends of the main street. Their instructions were to kill all whites except (curiously) Methodists, Frenchmen and Quakers. If they succeeded in taking Richmond, coordinated attacks were then to be made on other cities in the state.[5]

The plot failed. Before the attack could commence a sudden rainstorm inundated the roads and washed out vital bridges. In the meantime, two slaves betrayed the affair and the militia was called out. "They could scarcely have failed of success," a contemporary newsman wrote of the uprising, "for after all, we could only muster four or five hundred men, of whom not more than thirty had muskets." Gabriel Prosser's bold bid for freedom shook the slavocracy. Throughout the immediate countryside the white planters and families lived in continuing terror for their lives. A Virginia correspondent wrote to the (Philadelphia) *United States Gazette*: "Let but a single armed negro [*sic*] be seen or suspected, and, at once, on many a lonely plantation, there were trembling hands at work to bar the doors and windows that seldom had been even closed before, and there was shuddering when a gray squirrel scrambled over the roof, or a shower of walnuts came down clattering from the overhanging boughs."[6]

There was good reason for shuddering. In the Caribbean Toussaint L'Overture, the black ex-coachman who, through his extraordinary military genius, was to become the founder of the Republic of Haiti, had already decisively defeated 40,000 Englishmen in a slave revolt. He was soon to destroy the flower of the French army under no less a person than General Victor Le Clerc, Napoleon's illustrious brother-in-law. This turn of affairs in the Caribbean was indeed distressing to the Southern planters whose plantations teemed with thousands of sullen, resentful slaves. Did they know what was happening in the West Indies? *Could* they know?

They knew. In the very year of Gabriel Prosser's ill-fated insurrection at Richmond, a South Carolina slave called Denmark Vesey won a lottery and bought his freedom. His personal freedom was not enough. Vesey had experienced the horror of slavery, and he determined within himself that *every* man ought to be free. It is said that he refused to go to Africa at the urging of well-wishers because "he had not a will" to do so. He wanted to stay and see what he could do for his fellow creatures still in the snakepit of thralldom.

Vesey was an agitator. There is an interesting parallel between his life and that of the contemporary black nationalist, Malcolm X. Like Malcolm X he was "born to the system," and like Malcolm X he emancipated himself. Vesey, too, had a certain innate brilliance. He had traveled widely and was fluent in several languages. He was described as a "convincing talker," a natural leader who could move men to action. In the community where he lived he was both feared and respected.[7] Like Malcolm, he had a sense of manifest destiny, a belief that he was born to play a special role in history. And like the erstwhile disciple of Elijah Muhammad, he harbored a corrosive hatred for white men:

> Even whilst walking through the streets in company with another, he was not idle; for if his companion bowed to a white person he would rebuke him, and observe that all men were born equal, and that he was surprised that anyone would degrade himself by such conduct; that he would never cringe to the whites, nor ought anyone who had the feelings of a man. When answered, "We are slaves," he

would sarcastically and indignantly reply, "You deserve to remain slaves"; and if he were further asked, What can we do, he would remark, "Go and buy a spelling book and read the fable of Hercules and the Waggoner"; which he would then repeat, and apply it to their situation.[8]

For several months Vesey and his lieutenants quietly indoctrinated the Negroes of Charleston and the outlying plantations. The personal servant class was carefully avoided as consisting of Negroes who might give the conspiracy away out of loyalty to their white masters. "Take care," admonished Peter Poyas, one of the leaders, "not to mention it to those 'waiting men' who receive presents of old coats and such from their masters, or they will betray us." Together Vesey and Poyas perfected a highly secret leadership corps composed mainly of laborers, artisans, field hands, and certain officials of the Negro Methodist Church, none of whom had any close personal relations with the slavemasters. Each leader was responsible for a detail of men and for a specific assignment. The details of the conspiracy were known only to the cadre of leaders, and none of the rank and file knew any leader except the one assigned to him.

In the clandestine meetings held in neighboring swamps and forests, Vesey, who was acquainted with the French Revolution, strove to convince the slaves of their inherent right to freedom and to instill in them a sense of equality and a measure of self-confidence. He promised that, just as the Haitians, they could throw off the white man's yoke if they were willing to shed blood. Again like Malcolm X, he was adept in the use of the scriptures to show how God would deliver his people. But they must help themselves. They must strike the first blow. Vesey's plan was to set diversionary fires throughout the city of Charleston and, under cover of confusion, to seize the arsenals and naval stores. All whites who ran into the streets were to be massacred, including women, children and clergymen.

In spite of the elaborate precautions to maintain secrecy, the plot was discovered on the eve of its execution, and Vesey and his confederates were hanged. An estimated 9,000 slaves were involved in the affair. (Some contemporary reports say 50,000, but these were probably exaggerated by hysteria.) Thirty-five leaders were hanged. Thirty-seven others were sent outside the country. Both Vesey and Poyas died courageously, refusing under torture to name their confederates. With his last breath, Peter Poyas admonished his followers: "Do not open your lips! Die silent as you shall see me do."

When Nat Turner was born in Southampton County, Virginia, in 1800, his mother, an African-born slave, sought to kill him rather than see him reared in bondage. Turner grew up to be something of a mystic and a Baptist preacher. He thought that the Bible revealed a plan for the deliverance of his people from slavery, and that he had been chosen as the instrument of God to effect their rescue. "To be great," he declared, "I must appear so." Accordingly he "wrapped himself in mystery devoting his time to fasting and prayer." Turner dealt on the edge of the occult, and in various "experiments" sought to make paper, gunpowder and other things out of wood and metal. However, he enjoyed a certain respect in Southampton County—so much so that a white overseer permitted Nat to baptize him, to the great consternation and displeasure of other whites in the community.

After much fasting and prayer, the "spirit," he said, told him to "arise and prepare myself and slay my enemies with their own weapons." The "sign" which signaled the fullness of time was a solar eclipse in February of 1831. With four disciples Nat set out for the county seat of Jerusalem, after first massacring all the whites in his master's household. The little band picked up additional recruits along the way until they numbered about seventy. Moving under cover of darkness from plantation to plantation, they managed to kill fifty-five white men, women and children by dawn. When a white infant was spared, Turner ordered it killed with the warning: "Nits make lice." Only a poor white family which owned no slaves was spared.

Next day the alarm was sounded and the militia was ordered out to apprehend the slaves. Lerone Bennett describes the frenzy of military preparations in his book *Before the Mayflower*:

> By this time, soldiers were flocking to the county from all points. Three companies of artillery from Fort Monroe and detachments of men from the warships "Warren" and "Natchez" arrived. Hundreds of soldiers and militiamen from North Carolina and other Virginia counties thronged into the area. All in all, some three thousand armed men came to Southampton to put down the insurrection.[9]

It was now the white man's turn to do some bloodletting. Bennett says:

> A massacre followed. The enraged whites shot down innocent Negroes who smiled and innocent Negroes who did not smile . . . "Men were tortured to death, burned, maimed and subjected to nameless atrocities. The overseers were

called upon to point out any slaves whom they distrusted; and if any tried to escape they were shot down."[10]

Nat was caught eventually and hanged, along with sixteen others, but not before he created an atmosphere of panic throughout the Southeast. A contemporary writer reported that "fear was seen in every face; women pale and terror-stricken, children crying for protection, men fearful . . . but determined to be ready for the worst . . . we know not when or where the flame will burst forth . . . Some have died, others have become deranged from apprehension since the Southampton affair."[11]

The wealth of Newport and Boston, no less than that of Charleston and Savannah, was predicated upon the buying and selling of men. The exact number of men stolen from the African continent will never be known, but at least seven or eight million were imported into the continental United States, and untold millions of others were sold to the vast sugar plantations of the Caribbean. Since the mortality rate during the dreadful "middle passage" (the ship-board journey from slave stations on the African coast to the new world) ordinarily ranged from 30 to 50 percent, possibly half as many more were tossed to the sharks which trailed the slave ships for their grisly discards. It is little wonder that African culture declined, since for three centuries the flower of African manhood was cutting cane in Jamaica, picking cotton in Alabama or rotting at the bottom of the Atlantic Ocean. What is more, when slavery had finally run its course it was supplanted in Africa by colonialism and in America by apartheid, neither of which provided much opportunity for black men to make up the lost centuries given in involuntary service to the white man's civilization.

The captured blacks did not always wait until they were delivered in America to protest their loss of liberty. Many refused to eat, or refused to walk, and died or were killed in the coffles on the trip to the coast. Others starved or slashed themselves in the slave pens waiting for the slave ships to come. Others leaped from the boats ferrying them to the slavers waiting off shore. There was little chance of escape, but thousands drowned themselves or were eaten by sharks rather than accept slavery. An untold number revolted and died during the tortuous middle passage aboard ship, where they were chained between decks forty-eight inches high like so many swine. One slave who led a revolt and lived was Captain Tomba, bought from a slave pen in Sierra Leone. Described by John Atkins, a surgeon, as a handsome man "who scorned looking at us," Captain Tomba and a confederate later led a revolt aboard the slaver and killed three sailors before being subdued. The revolt was crushed, but "Captain Harding weighing the Stoutness and Worth of the two slaves [did] whip and scarify them only; while three others, Abettors but not Actors, nor of strength for it, he sentenced to cruel Deaths; making them first eat the Heart and Liver of one of them killed. The Woman he hoisted up by the Thumbs, whipped, and slashed her with Knives before the other slaves till she died."[12] Captain John Newton, who wrote the tender hymn "How Sweet the Name of Jesus Sounds," was master of such a slaver, holding prayer service twice a day for the benefit of the damned.

One of the celebrated sea revolts revolved around Cinque, a chief's son of the Mendi tribe of Sierra Leone. In the spring of 1839, Cinque was captured and sold to the Portuguese slaver "Tecora" which was in the slave trade with Cuba. Slave-trading in Spanish possessions had been outlawed officially, but continued clandestinely as an important commercial enterprise. The "Tecora" landed its cargo of slaves at an obscure village to which came slave dealers from Havanna who bought Cinque and forty-eight other men and three little girls. The new owners, Don Jose Ruiz and Don Petro Montez then chartered the ship "Amistad" ("Friendship") to deliver their slaves to the Cuban port of Guanje, three hundred miles east.

Four nights after the voyage was underway Cinque led the slaves in a revolt. The captain and his personal slave were killed. The other members of the crew were spared, but were put overboard in a small boat. Ruiz and Montez were held prisoner and were ordered to set sail for Africa. By a clever ruse the Cubans deceived the Africans and eventually brought the ship off the southern shore of Long Island where it was sighted by the Coast Survey ship "Washington." The Africans were recaptured and taken to New Haven, Connecticut, where they were imprisoned for the murder of the captain of the "Amistad." Their trial created an international stir, and contributed greatly to the widening rift between the North and the South over the slavery issue. Leading abolitionist lawyers of the day, including Governor William Ellsworth of Hartford, Roger S. Baldwin of New Haven, and former President John Quincy Adams, took up the cause of the Africans, and they were freed and returned to Sierra Leone—to the extreme discomfiture of President Martin Van Buren and the slave-holding South.

Negroes in slavery in both North and South protested

their condition whenever they could. But the weight of the law, the might of the armed forces, the disapproval of organized religion and the viciousness of revenge were everywhere employed to discourage any thoughts of freedom. The slaves had no allies except the Indians, who were themselves scheduled for extermination. But thousands of Negroes did escape to, and fuse with, the nearby Indian tribes throughout the whole of the slave period.

The savagery with which protest was punished is indicative of the fear engendered by the institution of slavery, and of the lengths to which the slaves were willing to go to free themselves. As early as 1687 a plot was uncovered in Virginia in which the slaves planned to kill all the whites during a mass funeral. John Hope Franklin writes that "before the end of the colonial period, Virginia, like her neighbors had become an armed camp in which the masters figuratively kept their guns cocked and trained on the slaves in order to keep them docile and tractable . . ." In Carolina in 1711, the slaves were described by the legislature as "keeping the inhabitants in great fear and terror." In 1739 there were three insurrections in Carolina, in one of which (the Cato conspiracy), the slaves secured arms and killed thirty whites while losing forty-four of their own number. Ten escaped to Florida and freedom. In 1741, an alleged plot between Negroes and poor whites to kill all the ruling whites in New York and establish a monarchy with a (poor) white king and a black governor produced a mass hysteria which resulted in the most brutal behavior on the part of the townspeople. Eighteen Negroes were hanged, thirteen burned alive and seventy banished. Four whites, including two women, were hanged. "At the rate of two every week, one hanged and one burned alive, the victims were executed amid prayers, imprecations and shrieks of agony."[13]

The fight for freedom was not always in the form of organized protest. On the plantations of the South murder was common, poison and ground glass being the favorite instruments. Many of the killers were women who took advantage of situations of intimacy to express their hatred of the masters and overseers who took advantage of their helplessness. But the killing of overseers and masters in the forests or in remote places of the plantations were also very numerous as the newspapers of the period indicate. Arson was another widely used form of protest, with houses, barns, forests and fields being put to the torch. Suicide and self-mutilation were frequent. Rather than work in the fields for the white man, slaves often cut off fingers or toes, and even hands and feet. In 1807 several hundred Negroes starved themselves to death at Charleston. Mothers frequently smothered their children to prevent their growing up in slavery.

Malingering, theft and sabotage were other forms of protest. Crops ready for harvest were frequently destroyed. Fences were broken to admit cattle and horses to growing crops, work stock killed, tools deliberately broken or lost, hogs poisoned or permitted to escape to the woods where they became wild.

Running away was perhaps the most readily available form of protest of all. As many as 100,000 slaves worth more than thirty million dollars escaped to the North via the "underground railroad" between 1810 and 1850 alone. Thousands of others escaped to the swamps and forests of the lower South where they were eventually absorbed by

the various Indian tribes. The Negro's proclivity to escape
was so strong that the medical journals of the period considered it a disease and gave it the name "monomania." Many
runaway Negroes formed isolated communities called "ma-
roons," which they defended and from which they staged
predatory raids upon neighboring plantations and towns.
One such maroon was hidden deep in the Dismal Swamp of
Virginia-North Carolina. Another was in Mobile County,
Alabama.

Organized protest often took the form of declarations
and petitions. In February of 1800, James Forten (who had
amassed a fortune of $100,000 as a sail-maker) and Absalom
Jones (an Episcopal priest) led the free Negroes of Philadelphia in submitting an anti-slavery petition to Congress. From
1830 on Negroes held a series of conventions to make reso-
lutions and otherwise address themselves to their peculiar
circumstances. Eventually these conventions were joined by
sympathetic whites like William Lloyd Garrison and Arthur
Tappan. As early as 1848 a convention meeting at Troy,
New York, urged Negroes to seek admission to white col-
leges, and in 1850 a convention at Columbus, Ohio, "resolved to resist all forms of oppression, promote universal
education, and encourage Negroes to mechanical, agri-
cultural and professional pursuits." A convention at Roches-
ter, New York, in 1853 gave birth to the National Council
of Colored People, a sort of nineteenth century NAACP.
The NCCP issued a memorial denouncing the universal mal-
treatment of the Negro people, but maintained a courageous
note of optimism in that in spite of the most formidable
handicaps, "we can without boasting, thank God, and take
courage, . . . [say we have] placed ourselves where we may

fairly challenge comparison with more highly favored men."

Individual protest among free Negroes of the North was loud and continuous. Many Negro orators like Charles Lenox Redmond and the great Frederick Douglass found a place for their talents in the Abolitionist Movement. There were others: Henry Highland Garnett, Martin R. Delaney (Harvard graduate, sometimes called the first black nationalist), Sojourner Truth, Harriet Tubman, James McCune Smith (M.D., University of Glasgow). John B. Russwurm (first Negro to earn a college degree—Bowdoin, 1826), and Samuel E. Cornish, a Presbyterian minister, founded the first Negro newspaper, *Freedom's Journal*, in 1827. David Walker, a free Negro of Wilmington, North Carolina, who had moved to Boston in 1828 ("If I stay in this bloody land [Carolina], I will not live long"), in 1829 published *Walker's Appeal*, an incendiary pamphlet denouncing the hypocrisy of slave-holding Christians and urging the slaves to rise up and "kill or be killed." Not all free Negroes were so radical. Then, as now there were voices urging "moderation" and "conciliation." Such a voice was that of Prince Hall, the founder of Negro masonry, whose counsel to his impatient brethren who were still enslaved was that they should "kiss the rod and be still, and see the works of God."

The convention movement survived the Civil War and continued through the Reconstruction, linking the "protest and progress" activities of the ante-bellum period with such counterpart organizations of today as the National Association for the Advancement of Colored People and the National Urban League. The Young Men's Progressive Association of New Orleans met in 1878; the convention of Colored Men of Texas convened in 1883. Macon, Georgia

had a Consultation Convention meeting in 1888, and the
National Afro-American League was formed in Chicago
in 1890.[14] But none of these prototype organizations was
able to counter effectively the hard matters of fact of Negro
existence in the United States, nor the deceptive skein of
myths woven with malevolent skill around the question of
the Negro's responsibility as a human being and his capacity
to function adequately in a civilized society.

As slavery became more profitable the slavocracy had
become concerned to offer a moral justification for the in-
human institution which produced its wealth and under-
girded its culture. At the same time, it sought to inculcate the
illiterate slaves (as it sought later to indoctrinate the freedmen and their erstwhile white supporters in the North) with
an image of the Negro designed shrewdly to discourage protest, and to encourage resignation and accommodation. This
was the "Magnolia Myth," so-called because it was usually
accompanied by a *Gone With the Wind* kind of phantasy
of banjo-strumming darkies lounging peacefully under the
sweet-scented magnolias behind the Big House, happy and
contented in their station, and forever loyal to the kind-
hearted master and his benevolent arrangement for their
mutual felicities. The Magnolia Myth explained the Negro's
condition in terms of his "natural docility," his "instinctive
servility," and his "inherent imbecility."

It alleged that the Negro's "docile nature" led to his
"willing" acceptance of bondage, and that his "instinctive
servility" made him an ideal slave—a being peculiarly
equipped psychologically to submit his will completely to
that of the white man, who sensed and accepted his own
inferiority, and who therefore desired that the use of his

body be at the disposal of the more moral and sophisticated will of his master. His imbecility derived, it was argued, from an inherent incapacity to be creative. The Negro race alone, it was said, had contributed nothing to the advancement of civilization, and the reason was that he was unable to progress mentally beyond the simple abilities of a child. This was a principal intent of the Magnolia Myth—to perpetuate an image of the Negro as being inherently inferior in intellect and therefore forever incapable of mastering the complex requirements of self-determination. The Negro was a child who could never grow up. Slavery was a "favor" to an incompetent race of people.[15]

After the cause of slavery had finally been settled by the Civil War, it was clear that if the South were to realize successfully its corporate intention to continue the economic and psychological exploitation of the Negro, it had to maintain and strengthen the myth of his innate inferiority. The institution of segregation, with its attendant ritual of deferential behavior, was the overt expression of the Magnolia Myth. Because the Negro had certain inherent, nay, *racial* incapacities, he was obviously a different order of being. His intellectual weakness, his stunted moral sense, his inability to dream great dreams (even dreams of freedom!) qualified severely his right (or his need) to have freedom of movement and freedom of self-determination in the American democracy. He would never be "ready." He must be "controlled," (i.e., segregated) for his own good and for the good of society.

Once the myth was fashioned, the historians, educators, novelists, politicians and a varied assortment of other myth-makers gave it currency. The law, the church and the school

gave it respectability. Science and history have discredited
the myth, but the continuing fact of Negro protest and Negro progress despite the universality of the myth provide its
most dramatic refutation. Today's Negro leadership is not
docile. Negro students involved in direct action are polite,
but hardly servile. Considering its successes before our
highest court, it is hard to believe that the legal staff of the
NAACP is a council of imbeciles.

The Magnolia Myth with its many ramifications remains a pervasive influence in our society. Our public in-
formation media, the textbooks our children use, our religious institutions have typically concerned themselves with
other interests. It has remained to the Negro to destroy the
myth himself.

The giant among Negro protest organizations is the
National Association for the Advancement of Colored
People. But if one is to be precise in definition, the NAACP
has never been a "Negro" organization. Of its initial founders, all three were white, one of the three being a Jew. What
is more, the initial statement laying the plight of the Negro
on the conscience of America came from the pen of a *Southern* white man, William English Walling. In a sort of open
letter to Americans published in the *Independent* following
the riot, Walling sought to invoke "the spirit of the abo-
litionists" to help alleviate the repressive conditions of the
Negro. "Who realizes the seriousness of the situation," he
demanded, "and what large and powerful body is ready to
come to their aid?" The law enforcement agencies were not.
That is patent, for in the 1908 riot that precipitated Walling's appeal, the Negroes of Springfield, Illinois, were driven

from their homes and out of the city *en masse*. Two were lynched, hundreds were beaten, scores of homes were burned, and Negroes employed by private employers and by the State of Illinois were summarily fired from their jobs. For what reason? A white woman beaten by her white lover tried to escape her husband's wrath by claiming to have been attacked by a Negro!

The Negro in America has always been a scapegoat. Times without number he has played the role of scapegoat for countless individuals who needed an alibi. But his larger function has been that of a *cultural* scapegoat. The sins of the society have been peremptorily thrown upon his shoulders and, like some black Atlas, he has borne them. But not without protest.

Joining William Walling in his concern to alleviate the Negro's condition were Mary White Ovington, a wealthy young humanitarian, and Henry Moskovitz, a social worker. Together they issued a call for a conference to be held in New York City in May of 1909. The call was written by Oswald Garrison Villard of the *New York Post*, and endorsed by many notables of the day, including John Dewey, John Haynes Holmes, W. E. B. Du Bois, Ida B. Wells Barnett and William Lloyd Garrison, among others. It said in part:

The celebration of the Centennial of the birth of Abraham Lincoln [Feb. 12, 1909] . . . will fail to justify itself if it takes no note of and makes no recognition of the colored men and women for whom the Great Emancipator labored to assure freedom. If Mr. Lincoln could revisit this country in the flesh he would be disheartened and discouraged. He would learn that on January 1, 1909 Georgia has rounded

out a new confederacy by disfranchising the Negro, after
the manner of all other Southern States ... that the Supreme
Court ... had refused ... to pass squarely on this disfran-
chisement ... that if an individual State chooses it may make
it a crime for white and colored citizens to frequent the
same market place ...

[He] would see black men and women set apart in trains in
which they pay first class fares for third class service ...
State after state declines to do its elementary duty in pre-
paring the Negroes through education for the best exercise
of citizenship. Added to this, the spread of lawless attacks
upon the Negro, North, South and West ... could but
shock the author of the sentiment that "government of the
people, by the people, and for the people, should not perish
from the earth."

Silence ... means tacit approval ... Hence we call upon all
believers in democracy to join in a National Conference for
... the renewal of the struggle for civil and political
liberty.[16]

The conference met on May 30, 1909, and absorbing
W. E. B. Du Bois' all black Niagra Movement, re-organized
as the National Negro Conference. At the second annual
conference a year later it became in turn the National Association for the Advancement of Colored People. So it has
been since—an organization of whites and Negroes, Christians and Jews, the purpose of which is to seek the "advancement" of the disadvantaged through democratic procedures
well established in the traditions of America:

To promote equality of rights and eradicate caste or race
prejudice among the citizens of the United States; to advance the interest of colored citizens; to secure for them

impartial suffrage; and to increase their opportunities for securing justice in the courts, education for their children, employment according to their ability, and complete equality before the law.[17]

So read the statement of incorporation.

The NAACP has relied traditionally upon "litigation, legislation and education" to produce the social changes which would ease somewhat the white man's burden the Negro had been carrying for so long. Its successes in winning key court cases affecting the Negro's right to vote, to avail himself of public education and housing, to exempt himself from jim crow practices in transportation, and such other interests has been phenomenal.

By 1913, a year in which there were seventy-nine lynchings, the NAACP had twenty-four branches and a national budget of $16,000. By 1963 the organization could boast of almost a half-million members from every walk of life. Lynching, a long-time target of NAACP activity, had all but disappeared. That year the organization spent a budget of well over a million dollars.

The recent presence of more activist-oriented organizations (like the Student Nonviolent Coordinating Committee) in the civil rights field has produced a certain defensiveness on the part of the NAACP. Litigation is sometimes long, usually slow and always expensive. Then too, once the courts have issued a favorable decree, there may still be months or years of evasion. Today's youth want instant freedom. They do not want to wait until tomorrow to "overcome." They want to overcome today. This is the way it *should* be. *Right* should not have to wait for *wrong's* convenience, especially having waited so long already. But things are seldom as they should be. Roy Wilkins, sagacious executive secretary of the NAACP, knows that if the fruits of direct action are to be preserved, they must be validated by law. Hence, he has shrewdly encouraged direct action by the students, backing them with financial support for bail, and sending the Association's lawyers to extricate them from the toils of Southern justice when things became a bit sticky. Quips Mr. Wilkins, "a bulldozer can make a proper excavation for a building, but it can't erect the steel." Despite the perfection of new techniques of protest, the main focus of the Association has remained where it always was—educating the people to accept social change, lobbying to effect legislative change, and seeking the repeal or re-interpretation of laws that seem racially unjust.

The National Urban League is not properly a "protest" organization, although it is frequently associated with the protest movement. This is primarily because the Urban League, having been organized about the same time (1910), is often thought of as the corollary of the NAACP. The two organizations are quite different in structure, goals, financing and leadership. Both the NAACP and the Urban League have interracial boards, both had white founders, and both are engaged generally in the business of improving the Negro's lot in America, but there the similarity ends. The NAACP is financed largely by membership fees, contributions and foundation grants. The Urban League depends upon local resources for the most part, and is in most cities a participating agency in the Community Chest. Hence, it is to some degree amenable to local sentiments.

Under the leadership of Whitney Young, who became

Executive Director in 1961, the League has changed radically. The image of extreme conservatism by which it has been known for most of its existence has been largely dissipated, and a pronounced dynamism has pervaded the organization. Mr. Young is a young man on the order of the John Kennedy school. He is a brilliant strategist and a sound planner. And he is pugnacious. For the first time in history responsible Negro leadership has the candor to admit that most Negroes are neither saints nor geniuses, and the temerity to insist that the Negro who is an average Joe has a right to a part of whatever the other average Joes in America are getting. In reacting to the white man's covert bigotry that hides behind his willingness to hire the "best" Negroes to work in his businesses (which are likely to be indiscriminate as to what Negroes or whites buy their products), Whitney Young discards the cringing apologeticism of the old professional Negro leaders and challenges the white man to racial introspection:

> Businessmen who have begun to open jobs to Negroes at levels they haven't before repeatedly say to us, "This person must be better than the average white. He's got to be 'Exhibit A.'"

> They were insisting, you know, that a secretary must be able to type 120 words a minute and look like Lena Horne, and that an accountant have the education of a Ralph Bunche. But after awhile the Negro runs out of Lena Hornes and Ralph Bunches.

> Any group, I suppose, runs out of these pretty fast. Management must now accept the qualified average Negro as they accept the qualified average white.

> In fact, I would go further to say that we also want man-

agement to give us some of those jobs they have set aside
for "dumb white people." We have some Negroes who are
not the brightest people in the world, and we need jobs for
them.[18]

From equal treatment for average people to preferential treatment for people whose opportunities have been
below average is a logical extension of Young's open-book
philosophy; but it is an extension fraught with dangerous
implications. Young takes the step in spite of criticism from
"friends" who wish him well. He believes that Negroes,
whose rate of unemployment is more than double that of
whites and whose skills are limited from a lack of incentive
to prepare for jobs they have never in the past been permitted to hold, should now be given some degree of preferential treatment in training and employment. Gunnar
Myrdal, the Swedish social scientist, has been one of the
liberal voices raised against "discrimination in reverse."
Myrdal suggests that preferential treatment for Negroes
would create hatred for them among other poor groups.
Mr. Myrdal is right, of course. It is also true that except for
existing hatred among "other groups" irrespective of economic status, the Negro would not today be in need of preferential treatment. But I cannot agree with Young when he
says that because of the Negro's political leverage the poor
white should "keep quiet" and try to "ride in on the coat-
tails of the Negro."[19] The Negro spent most of his century
of "freedom" trying to hitch a ride on this or that set of coat-
tails. It was only after he decided to *get himself a coat* that
he got anywhere.

Except for the short-lived and ill-starred Populist

Movement, Negroes and poor whites have had little inclination and less success in working together. Not that they
should not—nothing is more logical. But of course race prejudice is not logical. The Negro masses and the poor whites
occupy essentially the same class. They would have a vast
commonality of interests except for the fact that the poor
white has been taught that whatever he has in common with
the Negro—poverty, illiteracy, oppression—is outweighed
by the factor of race. They cannot work together until the
white man learns, or until he is forced to accept, the fact
that a pale skin is in the final analysis a rather empty value.

Another thing is implied in Whitney Young's admo-
nition to whites to "keep quiet," but probably not in his conscious meaning at the time. This is the Negro's historic contempt for poor whites—something they learned from the
slavemasters and never forgot, "ain't nothing lower than
poor white trash." And in this era of status-seeking within
and without the caste arrangement, one of the most frustrating aspects of being a Negro is to be looked down upon and
segregated by people "who don't know you're better than
they are." Only the Muslims have been forthright about
feeling superior to anybody white, and they have been
properly drowned out in a loud chorus of brotherhood. But
the Negro needs to be aware of his own prejudices and hos-
tilities if he is serious about democracy.

The Urban League's new image is refreshing. *Some
whites are going to be alienated.* Possibly the League will lose
some financial support. Be that as it may. In presenting the
issues without embellishment, and in facing his critics (and
his supporters) with statesman-like candor, Mr. Young is
bringing to Negro leadership a new kind of dignity. More

than that, he is offering the white man respect and the chance
to be respectable. The obsequious tomism that characterized
"communication" between whites and Negroes for so long
is dead. Both whites and Negroes should rejoice in noting
its obituary. It was degrading to them both.

> I think the white community makes a real mistake in re-
> minding the Negro of the possibility of alienating white
> people because he pushes for his rights.

> A Negro mother whose husband is unemployed, whose
> children are bitten by rats, who is living in a house without
> heat, couldn't care less about alienating some white person.

> And to suggest to the Negro that "I will be your friend
> only so long as you let me decide on the pace at which you
> are to receive your rights" irritates the Negro to no end. It
> says that rights that are God-given and that are constituion-
> ally decreed can be withheld or can be given by another
> human being. And we don't think that this is true.

> So, if it alienates white people to have Negroes given rights
> that white people have always enjoyed, then the Negro
> says: "I'm sorry. He'll just have to be alienated."[20]

This is Whitney Young of the National Urban League.
He is communicating the new image of responsible Negro
leadership. America might well take time out to listen to
what he is trying to say, for the inevitable alternative will
be less pleasant and more costly in the long run.

A protest movement is a symptom of pervasive social
conflict distorting the normal social relations between dis-
crete groups of people. It is an expression of the deep anxiety
and discontent of one group reacting against what is perceived as the abuse of power by some other group. Power

is the control over decisions. A protest movement is a reaction protesting that control or the character of its expression.[21]

Direct action protest has become an important means
of communicating the Negro's extreme dissatisfaction with
his condition of existence in America. Scores of bombings,
beatings, and shootings have brought death to any number
of Negroes under circumstances relating to racial protest,
but the protests have continued unabated. The Negro is trying desperately to say something to America. The Federal
Bureau of Investigation has been notoriously ineffective in
bringing to justice the murderers and other criminals who
have abandoned completely civilized procedures in a vain
but persistent attempt to intimidate civil rights protest. But
FBI Director J. Edgar Hoover has complained petulantly
about "communist infiltration" in the civil rights movement.
It is worth noting in passing that the FBI is in great danger
of losing the confidence of Negroes and other fair-minded
Americans who may come to suspect it of being one more
example on the long and weary list of institutionalized prejudice. There is tragedy implicit in such a possibility, for "we
must not," as Shakespeare warned, "make a scarecrow of the
law." But where there is but little confidence there cannot
be great respect.

There is national concern today over the fact that Negroes have taken their protests into the streets. Well there
may be, for the streets are conducive to anarchy. The formality of the law is sobering—even when the law is unjust
and the dignity of the conference table assuages the passions,
even when the conference is a spurious clamor of quiet fury

signifying nothing. The white man does not understand the Negro's protest because he thought the Negro had capitulated generations ago. The Negro slave did not capitulate; he merely resigned himself to what he could not change, but he did not *accept* his status as being either moral, inevitable or permanent. The slave communicated his expectation of deliverance in his spirituals and his folk tales. The white man heard what the slave was saying, but because of his own arrogance and his irrevocable commitment to a slave economy, he was unable to make a moral response. To the white man, the freedom and the equality of the slave were inconceivable categories. So it is today. With rare exception even the most dependable white liberals do not honestly concede the Negro's equality. Equality before God, yes. Equality before the law, probably. But equality as a *person* of worth entitled to participate in *all* the common values of this society without restriction, hardly. These are not pseudo-liberals, or "fickle phonies" as they are known to their Negro critics. These are white men and women who have a genuine desire to see the Negro's status improve, but not to a degree commensurate with their own. The so-called "backlash" of anti-Negro sentiment revealed in the North through the campaigns of Alabama's Governor Wallace was largely a mass reaction to the perceived threat of Negro equality in the North.

The Negro and the white man have each moved through a progression of relationships *vis-à-vis* each other. First there were masters and slaves; then citizens and "freedmen"; and finally citizens and "second-class citizens." In the first relationship, the white man owned whatever there was in the slave that could be reduced to property values and protected by law. Later, the Emancipation Proclamation, the successful conclusion of the Civil War and the Thirteenth Amendment brought "freedom" to all Negroes then in bondage, and the Fourteenth Amendment conferred upon them the right to vote. The right to vote did not long enhance the freedman's status in the society. In less than a generation his right to vote was qualified' most severely, and although he was able to retain that right as an abstract principle of constitutional law, the opportunity to exercise it was scarcely afforded him after 1878.

Hence, the Negro's "citizenship" was defective from the beginning and this fact has important overtones in the civil rights struggle today. In the mind of the white man, the Negro remains "different," and this difference acts to modify the law and the protection of the law as it applies to him. The fundamental principles of law which have everywhere operated to protect and guarantee the preeminence of citizens in their own country have never in the history of America given full or even reasonable protection to the Negro. Not only have his rights and privileges been the perpetual playthings of American bigots and scofflaws, but his "citizenship" has generally afforded him less protection and respect than the white skin of any foreigner—even *black* foreigners traveling or resident in this democratic commonwealth. That is what Negro protest is all about; and that is the meaning and significance of Malcolm X, who stalks ominously in the wings of this sick-sick society.

The progression of relationships between white men and black men has come finally to the stage of citizens and "second-class citizens." Second-class citizenship has no meaning. It is a logical contradiction. It is at best a euphemism for the political limbo between being a freedman with limited rights, and being a citizen with the same rights all other citizens have. For a hundred years the Negro has accommodated himself to a role-image designed by the white man to enhance his own sense of personal worth, and to preserve his own economic advantage. As is characteristic of accommodative relationships, communication between Negroes and whites has for that hundred years been highly restricted and uniquely ceremonial. The white man has "heard" only what is consistent with the ideological presuppositions of white supremacy. The Negro has heretofore accommodated himself to the white man's self-image by reciting to the white man the words the white man taught him to say and wished him to believe. Obviously, there was no viable communication; no transfer of ideas took place. The white man went on believing what he heard the Negro say, and it was expedient for the Negro to go on saying what the white man wanted to believe. The corollaries of such an unhealthy relationship were evasion, deception, and the postponement of the inevitable denouement we are witnessing today.

The Congress of Racial Equality (CORE), the Student Nonviolent Coordinating Committee (SNCC or "SNICK"), Martin Luthern King's Southern Christian Leadership Conference (SCLC) and their counterparts have taken the issues into the streets. The present relationship is not accommodative; it is accusative, defiant and essentially revolutionary. It is also explosive, at least potentially. But it does assure meaningful communication. Under an accommodative relationship communication was negated for two principle reasons: (1) The Negro spoke from weakness rather than strength. Noting this, the white man's response was patronizing and paternalistic rather than equalitarian. (2) Where the Negro dared to be assertive rather than supplicative, he did not speak directly to the white man, but to his institutions, i.e., to the legal, religious and economic entities which stand between the white man and the consequences of his behavior. The NAACP won case after case in the courts but, since this was the confrontation of an institution (the *laws* requiring segregation, not the *people* doing the segregating), communication was indirect and its effectiveness was to some degree vitiated. It was the "bad laws" that were under attack, not bad people. The law is an abstraction. It is *of* the people, or *by* the people, but it is not the people. Ideas *may* be exchanged through the medium of the law, to be sure, but the import and meaning of the exchange is often absorbed by the courts and the enforcement agencies, and may never reach the people at all. As a consequence, the white man's response to the Negro's "legal communication" has been made in turn "to the courts," or to "judge-made law" or "sociology" or some other abstraction. Until this era of active protest, with some minor deference to the law, the white man has been able to maintain his studied obliviousness to the Negro as a person and as a citizen.

Direct action techniques—sit-ins, protest marches, freedom rides, selective buying campaigns, etc., have ushered in a new category of relationships. Communication between the races has never been better than it is today. The widespread lamentation over the "breakdown of communication" in the South (and in the North) results from a very grievous misinterpretation of what is involved in social communication. What is actually being lamented is the demise of a superficial "cordiality" which has illustrated the ceremonial approach to race relations. Americans are still surreptitiously committed to the comforting idea that the white man "knows" the Negro: what he is, what he wants, what he needs and how he will behave under specified circumstances. This sophistry is self-deluding. Like benevolent paternalism and the rest of the familiar pattern of condescension, it is the product of a vast racial ego which feeds on self-deceit. The white man does not "know" the Negro, has never known him and has never undertaken seriously to find out what he is like as a person. It is patent that in a caste society the members of the upper caste are prohibited by the very nature of the caste proscriptions from the kind of contact and the interchange of ideas which would enable them to know anything meaningful about the lower caste. For most of the history of America the white man has considered the Negro to be a different order of being altogether—another species of animal, scarcely capable of the white man's idealized moral and cultural pretensions. This fundamental absurdity alone has constituted an impregnable barrier to an intelligent assessment of the Negro as a human being.

There has been no breakdown in communication because responsible communication between the races did not exist until the Negro abandoned the ceremonies of the old arrangement and began speaking directly to the white man, expressing his *true* feelings and underscoring his attitudes with overt, illustrative behavior. The white man's response has often been one of bewilderment, chagrin and fear. He is bewildered because he has come to believe his own dogma. He honestly thought he *knew* the Negro. What he really knew was the image of the Negro that he himself had created. To wake up to another reality has been, on occasion, like a very bad dream. His chagrin stems from self-delusion, but it seems to him that it is the Negro who has deceived him by assuming a strange and hostile role which does not complement his own self-image. His fear and anxiety are natural responses to being caught offguard at a crucial moment in history.

For the first time the white man has begun to listen to what the Negro has been trying to tell him, and he is required by a new set of circumstances to make a non-perfunctory response. This is a healthy impasse to which we have now come. The white man's deliberate ignorance of the Negro as a person and of his aspirations as a citizen has been destroyed. From this point forward the only alternatives to the practice of equality will be the expulsion of the Negro or his annihilation. Since such extremes are not viable in a Christian democracy, it would seem that a reconstruction in race relations is at hand. Negroes will be legal equals and will be treated as such. The expression of the democratic ideal will at last approximate the spirit and intent of the law.

The true equalitarian society is somewhat more distant. Because an enlightened society always sets its highest moral values beyond its legal expectations, the millennium cannot come with the mere observance of legal justice. To be sure, legal justice is a very significant attainment in the maturation of a society. At a minimum, it guarantees that every man will receive what is his due, thereby assuring the equality of citizens before the law. But legal justice and social morality are not necessarily the same thing, and at this point in our development, neither the white man nor his black counterpart offers any evidence of the moral maturity that looks very far beyond legal justice. Indeed, we have come but lately to the threshold from which we are willing to contemplate seriously the simple legal axiom of rendering to every man his due.

The new communication which has evolved between blacks and whites has not come without bitterness and hostility. Thousands of Negroes who have been engaged in communicating with the white man through direct action have been brutally assaulted. In Birmingham, Alabama, fire hoses and vicious dogs were turned upon Negro demonstrators who wanted no more than to make known their attitudes toward segregation. In Jackson, Mississippi, convicts were used to throw scores of Negroes into foul-smelling garbage trucks to be hauled off to makeshift compounds like so many swine. The crime which brought about so brutish an attempt at humiliation was the Negroes' peaceful protest against discrimination. *The irony of it all is that Negroes confronting the white man today refuse to be humiliated.* In Jackson, they accepted the garbage trucks and prayed for the white men who preferred to abuse them rather than to hear what they had to say about freedom. They were trying to convey to the white people of Jackson that in the minds of the Negro masses, segregation is more contemptible than a ride in a garbage truck. The racial dialogue can be dangerous: some Negroes engaged in it have been murdered, and the number of killings will probably continue to mount as the situation becomes more acute.

"Moderates" in both racial camps tend to be more concerned over whether Negroes and whites hate each other than they are over the resolution of the issues. This concern reflects a genuine passion for the common realization of the moral values implicit in the American Creed. To the "moderate," it does not seem rational that in an advanced Christian democracy citizens who have worked together, fought together, worshipped the same God (albeit in separate congregations!) and known each other so intimately for so many generations could suddenly have developed a consuming hatred for each other. Of course, the presuppositions of any who think in these terms are faulty to begin with. Our racial "togetherness" has been essentially fictional. We have worked, fought, and even lived *side by side*, but seldom "together." We have indeed worshipped the same God but our prayers and expectations have been based upon different perspectives.

The unhappy truth is that hatred is an integral part of any caste society, and the more strict the observance of the forms which hold the system together, the more intense the hatred is likely to be. It is inevitable that the intense hostility and resentment accumulated through generations of preserving (or attacking) the American caste system will express itself in increasing violence. The alternative is the development of measures to accomplish rapid desegregation which obviate direct and hostile confrontation between blacks and whites who have disparate values at stake.

Social conflict within a consensual framework may be functional, of course, for consensus precludes the emergence of the uncontrolled violence which ignores the rules and the weapons of the consensus. Where consensus is not present, conflict may be extremely dysfunctional. The danger in relying upon direct action techniques for example, lie in the possibility of assuming consensus where there is none. This is what precipitated the riot in Birmingham. The "rules" of

the protest demonstrations had been clearly established in
scores of sit-ins and wade-ins and prayer marches throughout the South over the past several years. Each racial faction
in Birmingham knew what was expected of it by the other.
The intentions of the demonstrators were prominently an-
nounced in the press and through radio and television. But
there was no consensus. The white police descended upon
the marchers with dogs and fire hoses. White hoodlums
bombed homes and businesses in the Negro community. The
Negroes responded with assaults upon white persons, and
burning and pillaging. None of these activities was within
the rules of consensus.

There is no reason to believe that more serious violence
will not erupt in the absence of very positive measures on the
part of the federal government or some other agency capable
of emancipating the Negro from the shackles of prejudice
and discrimination. The proliferation of "nonviolent" attacks upon Southern institutions has resulted in a situation
of increasing anxiety for the Southern white man who per-
ceives them as a threat to the values he has identified with life
itself. But the Negro's anxieties increase too, for the nearer
he approaches his goal the more elusive it seems to become.

There is a long history of violence in the South. Among
whites, it has ranged from the genteel violence of dueling
through the "feuding" of the lower classes to the barbarism
of lynching. Among Southern Negroes, the rate of crimes
of violence is higher than for any other sub-group in the
country. Much of the Negro's aggression has been displaced upon other Negroes, but assaults against whites are
increasing in frequency. The Black Muslim philosophy has
deeply permeated some segments of the Negro community,

but even if this were not so, as true sons of the South Negroes are by no means nonviolent by nature.

As more whites are able to break with the undemocratic ways of thinking and acting which characterized the relationships between the races in the past, and as more Negroes are admitted to the enjoyment of the common values of citizenship, racism as a philosophy will decline, as will the hatred endemic to our caste system. There is already some evidence that many white people, including some Southerners, are daring to see some Negroes as being essentially like themselves. This is a healthy sign for America. Some whites and some Negroes will never overcome their racial hatred because a need to feel superior is integral to their basic personality structures. Some well-meaning moderates would solve the problem by turning the South into another North. God forbid. That is not the answer. The only lasting solution is complete equalitarianism, the equalitarianism that gives a man the right to be black, or white, or any other color and still enjoy the full benefits of citizenship. Now that Negroes and whites have begun talking to each other on a serious level, that which has been a dream for so many generations *could* become a reality tomorrow. But the millenium is not yet. There are other factors to consider which may yet bring America to the supreme test of the principles which have made her great, and the visions which may make her free.

Chapter 3

MOOD EBONY:
The Acceptance of Being Black

What is my disease?
Tell me.
Who can name my crime?
Is it only that I am black
And not white?[1]

A quarter of a century ago W. E. B. Du Bois, then teaching sociology at Atlanta University, complained bitterly about the white man's unwillingness to recognize the Negro genius. Commenting on the rewriting of history to fit the Negro image that had been conjured out of the white man's guilt over long centuries of black slavery, Du Bois declared:

The whole attitude of the world was changed to fit this new economic reorganization. Black Africa, which had been a revered example to ancient Greece and the recognized contender with imperial Rome, became a thing beneath the contempt of Modern Europe and America. All history, all science was changed to fit this new condition. Africa had no history. Wherever there was history in Africa or civilization, it was of white origin; and the fact that it was civilization proved that it was white. If black Pharaohs sat on the throne of Egypt, they were not really black men but dark white men. Ethiopia, land of blacks, was described as a land of whites. If miracles of art appeared on the West Coast these were imported from artless Portugal. If Zymbabwe, with mines and irrigation appeared in the East, it was wholly Asiatic. If at any time, anywhere there was evidence in Africa of the human soul and the same striving of spirit and the same build of body found elsewhere in the world, it was all due to something non-African and not to the inherent genius of the Negro race.[2]

There has never been a Negro born in America who has not been crippled and maimed by the great lie of racial inferiority. That such is the case is patent at first consideration, but the subtle ramifications of the obvious fact are more difficult to perceive, even by Negroes themselves. Many Negroes are sufficiently accommodated to the racial *rapprochement* as to be superficially oblivious of its more serious detriments. A small number of others have by popular acclaim or professional attainment managed to escape to a limited degree the consummate detrition of personality and human worth which is the inevitable accompaniment of being a Negro in America. But there is no escape for the masses, and even for those who feel themselves emancipated there is the lurking fear of someday finding their emancipation to be a dream that has been shattered with a single word or gesture.

The self-hatred engendered by the caste constrictions is intense. In the lower classes it is expressed as displaced aggression upon other Negroes. In the middle and upper classes it is projected outward as hatred for Caucasians (especially Jews) and lower-class Negroes. In his study of the psychology of the Negro, Bertram P. Karon[3] finds that the lower-class Negro, in order to control his anger and resentment, "engages in various sorts of compensatory behavior: flashy dressing, denial of Negro attributes, narcosis (alcohol),

... gambling, and explosive spending." Though emotionality is somewhat improved in the middle and upper classes, Karon observes that

> ... nearly all of that is cancelled out by the pressure for status. . . . They drive themselves harder, and refuse the compensatory activities of the lower class. They are vulnerable to depressed self-esteem, and have a harder time with the control of anger. . . . Their guilt over hatred of other Negroes, plus a fear of retaliation, leads to a "success phobia." They also overshoot the mark of conformity to the white ideals . . . [and] their feelings of worthlessness may take the form of an unconscious identification with feces ...

In an independent analysis cited in Kardiner and Ovesey's classic study of the destructive effects of segregation on the Negro personality,[4] the following conclusions were drawn:

> ... a summary of ratings of intellectual status . . . indicates that all the subjects are assayed as average or better. However, 92% of the group give evidence of reduced efficiency and incomplete utilization of potential capacity.

> Profound anxiety is hypothesized in all the records. Life is viewed as dangerous, hostile, and assaultive. They feel small and inferior; and they have a persistent fear of mutilation and destruction.

> Another universal trait in this group is their inability to give free rein to their assertive and aggressive drives and destructive impulses. These impulses are a source of conflict and disability; and they are not accepted complacently. The subjects are tense and strained and they sit uncertainly on the lid of a turbulent and explosively simmering cauldron of hostility. They expend great energy in containing and con-

trolling aggression. Yet, always, it remains a problem to them.

The control of his aggressive tendencies and the accommodation to the white man's persistent image of what the Negro is or ought to be amount to the same thing. The Negro has been bottled up like some high explosive for generations. The present concern seems variously to be to de-fuse him by discrediting his leaders; de-activate him by controlled detonation, such as the march on Washington; or render him *im*plosive rather than *ex*plosive by suffocating his organizations with well-meaning moderates. There does not appear to be anywhere any serious general intention of accepting him as a person without qualifications which ultimately reflect the racial prejudices we claim to have forgotten.

The myth-makers have done their work well. Self-hatred has scarred the Negro personality like some corrosive acid. No sane man can marvel that this is so, because for all his life in America the Negro has been hated for being black and he has learned from his haters to hate himself. Harold Isaacs, a Jewish scholar whose empathy for the Negro's emotional struggle has the peculiar keenness and perception common to some Jews who have been able to extrapolate the sufferings of their own people, writes poignantly of "reaching back to take the hand of that . . . lonely [Negro] child and hear again his cry of pain and anger at being taken for "*cannibal, evil, black African* . . ." Being of "cannibal, evil, and black African" descent, the Negro aspirant's hopes for acceptance and meaningful participation in this society were precluded before ever he saw the light of day. Far more devastating was the fact that he could not hope, and nowhere in his hated ancestry could he find an image to make his ideal. His only reference was the white man, and white America alternately greeted his bumbling efforts to be a black white man with benign tolerance or with outright derision, or else ignored him altogether. "I am prepared to say," Isaacs writes,

> . . . that the systematic debasement, and self-debasement of the Negro in this white world has . . . been underpinned by the image the Negro child has gotten of the naked, savages, uncivilized African. . . . It is the picture of his contemporaneous ancestor which for generation after generation, has stared out at every Negro child who did get to school from nearly the first book he held in his hands. At a given moment of great and fearful and wondering interest he turned the pages of the geography text from which he was to learn the nature and shape of the world, and there . . . was the portrait of his origins, the picture of himself, the reason (as the text often inferred or flatly said) for his lowly backwardness and dim prospects.[5]

"The Picture" is a universal experience in the life of Negro Americans. It is the picture of a black savage with a bone through his nose, hoops in his ears and discs in his lips. There are feathers around his knees, and circulets around his ankles. His teeth are filed to points, and his face is horribly marked with tribal scars. His countenance sags under the weight of ignorance and stupidity. And he is black, black, *black*! This is the representation of the black race—the people who have "contributed nothing" to civilization.

We need not here dignify such nonsense with a digression for the purpose of rebuttal. It will suffice to say that those who need it may have it for themselves. What is significant is that a hundred years of solid Negro achievement under the most harrowing circumstances is a persistent *de facto* rebuttal, and the contemporary black revolution argues forcefully for a reassessment of history.

America claims surprise and disbelief at the depth of the revolution which is wracking our cities and threatening the carefully institutionalized values and taboos which have given us our characteristic image as a two-caste democracy. There is of course an obvious paradox inherent in the existence of a democratic caste system, but we have lived with it so long that to be called now to re-examine its postulates seems rude beyond forgiveness. The tragedy is that we do not really recognize what the revolution is about or what is at stake in it. We keep asking the Negro leaders, "What do 'your people' want now?" "When will they be satisfied?" The leaders can no more say what the people want than America can give it to them in a civil rights bill. What the people want is to some degree ineffable. It defies articulation in terms of objectives that can be enumerated or specified. Some have called it "dignity," but no nation can bestow dignity upon its citizens. Men can only dignify themselves. That is part of what the revolution is about—the denial of the "Big Lie"; the repudiation of "The Picture"; the challenges of a spurious history. The Negro leaders talk about jobs, and housing, and better schools and voting rights. Yes. All this too. These are the minimum objectives; and despite the long, long, century of denial, they are the things America can give most easily. It is so much harder to relinquish an idea than a thing or a privilege.

Columbia University Professor Daniel Bell, writing in the *New York Times* magazine,[6] is—like many other Americans—baffled by the proliferation of Negro leaders and the multiplicity of objectives they seem to be pursuing. "There are," Professor Bell insists, "two preconditions for successful political bargaining in the American system":

> One is that the Negro community has to choose its political spokesmen in a responsible way (in the way the farm groups have done); the other is that the Negro community has to specify its priorities and demands so that we know what to bargain about. In short there has to be a consensus about the ends desired—and such a consensus is not simply a list of slogans.

Obviously Professor Bell is confused as to the nature of the revolution. Or perhaps he is not convinced that there is one. The kids in the streets of Cambridge, Maryland and St. Augustine, Florida are not fighting to raise the price of ham a few cents. *They are involved and their lives are involved in changing the social structure of America!* There *is* a revolution going on, call it by another name or not; and while the goals and objectives are not always finely delineated or articulated with clarity and consistency, they are, or they will be discovered to be, goals of ultimate value rather than such immediate values as jobs and housing. The college students who risk their lives in voter registration efforts in Mississippi or in the picket lines in Tuscaloosa know that they are engaging in something of greater breadth and depth than a simple campaign to persuade the white man to let some Negroes vote, or eat at a public lunch counter. Their young white allies know it too. They have not come south to risk their lives for the sake of an integrated hamburger, but because they see that beyond the hamburger and beyond the ballot box their country is in trouble. It is right and just that the Negro should have his hamburger and his ballot, but the critical issue is how to change the basic presuppositions responsible for their being withheld in the first place.

It is probable that Professor Bell speaks for a growing number of white people (and not a few middle-class Negroes) when he complains about the proliferation of Negro leaders of questionable ability and about what seems to be a sharp increase in "militancy." The professor illustrates his own impatience with a quote from another writer in the *New York Times* who said that, "Almost every week a new civil rights organization is born ... and another man or woman is acclaimed as a civil rights leader ... Experience, education and social standing are not necessary for this leadership. What is necessary is the ability to articulate the desperate feelings of the impatient members of the community." Doubtless, it would be reassuring if all of the protest leaders could be chosen by ballot, and if only well-bred, educated men and women with "social standing" could qualify as candidates for leadership. It would be pleasant too if, once these "leaders" were chosen, they could sit down with their counterparts in the white community and negotiate the end of racial discrimination in America. But too many "well-bred, educated" Negroes are too busy trying to maintain precisely that image to be found where the action is— on the picket lines, and the "well-bred, educated" whites sit silently by on their suburban patios where no Negroes are —yet. The bombing and the head-smashing isn't being done by the "best" white people, and the "best" Negroes would rather not offend anyone lest they jeopardize the tenuous approbation they have laboriously earned for behaving themselves.

For the first time in recent history the Negro is choosing his own leaders. When his primary concern was to accommodate to the prevailing order, the white man chose the Negro's leaders and imposed them upon the black community. From time to time, various enterprising individuals with a sense of mission (or a scent of money) have represented themselves as "leaders" and have so presented themselves to the White Establishment with varying degrees of success. In fact, the would-be leadership of the tortured black caste has run the gamut from the brilliant intellectuals like Du Bois to the latest Johnny-come-lately with nothing more than his "militance" to recommend him. But the people have not followed all who presumed to lead. In his plea for a new phase in Negro leadership, Professor Bell articulates the concern among careful students of social change that the protest movement is heading for an explosion. He also articulates the anxiety of leaders like Whitney Young, who work within the established consensus, that too many distractions obscure the main issues with which we shall ultimately have to deal.

From another perspective the proliferation of leadership is an unmistakable sign of the revolutionary spirit which is energizing the Negro masses. As the volcano bubbles and seethes, new leaders will continue to be spewed up. The vast majority of them will be, in the words of the poet, "like snow upon the desert's dusty face, lighting a little hour or two" before passing on into obscurity. But out of this process will come the leadership that is truly representative of the people, and ultimately this is the leadership with which America must make its peace. Perhaps that leadership is already on the scene: it may be a man with a methodical plan,

such as Whitney Young; or a man with a dream, such as
Martin Luther King; or an apostle of nonviolence, such
as James Farmer; or a flaming radical, such as Malcolm X, or
a black apostle, such as Elijah Muhammad. The point is that
whoever leads the Negro people from this point on will be
someone that they themselves have chosen. This will be a
good thing. They may, of course, make mistakes, as other
people looking for quick and easy solutions to complex problems of social change have made mistakes. Indeed, there is
no guarantee that they may not follow a man on a white
horse (or more likely, a black horse!) a long way down the
wrong road. There is ample precedent in history.

One of the most significant achievements to come out
of the whole Negro protest is that in striving for the white
man's acceptance, the black man has learned to accept himself. In a society oriented completely to the white man's
value construct, this is an accomplishment of no little moment. The Negro's self-acceptance is far from being universal, of course, but it is clearly illustrated in the new ideas
he has about himself—and his new behavior, while not characteristic, is indicative of a trend. The *mood ebony*, this new
feeling about himself that is expressed in the acceptance—
even the glorification—of being black in a white man's world,
has challenged the Negro before, but never so deeply or at
a level that is both emotional and intellectual. When Marcus
Garvey, that Africanesque little Jamaican, came screaming
out of the Caribbean after the First World War, his doctrine
of black nationalism was an emotional panacea for the black
masses of America who were shaken and confused by the
white man's summary rejection of their notion that the
world they had fought to make safe for democracy some

how included them. In the midst of the unprecedented wave
of lynchings and race riots that signaled America's return to
normalcy, Garvey's constant reminder that Negroes were
persons of value did more than he was ever given credit for
to relieve the mass frustrations of a shocked and disappointed
people. In *The Negro World*, the propaganda organ for his
movement,

> Garvey proudly recalled for his followers, though not
> always with complete accuracy, the stirring heroism of such
> leaders of American slave rebellions as Denmark Vesey,
> Gabriel Prosser, and Nat Turner. The struggles of Zulu
> and Hottentot warriors against European rule, the histories
> of Moorish and Ethiopian empires, and the intrepid exploits
> of Toussaint L'Overture against the French in Haiti were
> not neglected in the effort to make Negroes conscious and
> proud of their racial heritage.[7]

At the height of his movement, Garvey had possibly
two or three million Negroes enrolled in his Universal Negro Improvement Association. "Up, you mighty race!" he
thundered. "You can accomplish what you will." The Negro masses were impressed. They wanted desperately to believe in Marcus Garvey's reconstruction of the Negro past,
and his grand dream for the black man's future. They
wanted to be black men because they were rejected by white
men. And they bought a dream in Africa because, in the
American Dream, they always woke up screaming.

The Negro intelligentsia wanted no part of Garvey's
black nationalism and no share in his dream of redemption
in Africa. Africa was still a nightmare to them, a land of ignorance, savagery, and above all, *blackness*. "Blackness" not
merely as a skin color, but as a philosophy, a way of life.

Blackness was the antithesis of whiteness, and whiteness was synonymous with culture—culture, progress and acceptance. *Acceptance*. Surely the white man would accept them some day if they learned carefully to duplicate his behavior, his manners, his morals and his ideals. In his revealing study entitled *The New World of Negro Americans*,[8] Harold Isaacs of the Massachusetts Institute of Technology probes the hidden recesses of some well-known Negro personalities "who have crashed through the 'big gate' from the Negro world into the larger white world beyond." Without exception their attitudes toward Africa are either negative or very carefully guarded. Here are some samples of responses made to Isaacs on questions about Africa:

> As a child I remember my mother and father talking about African classmates they had at college, they were brown, Moroccans—not black.

> My interest in Africa came late and is still limited, not only limited, but I have numerous inadequacies on this. When I was working on my lectures and writings, I had to work very hard at it. I have great difficulties in sustaining my interest and retaining knowledge about Africa or any part of it.

> I suppose I shared the general vague picture Americans had, and I suppose still have: a place by our standards backward, uncivilized . . . I have no sense of any tie between me and Africa.

> I had an aunt who . . . when kids got out of hand would say: "You little black Africans" or "you little fuzzy headed Africans!" She herself was quite light.

> The worst thing anyone could say to you in addition to calling you "black nigger" was "black African."

Garvey's movement was foredoomed to failure. In the first place his back-to-Africa plans were neither conceived soundly, planned with thoroughness nor executed effectively. Further, the task Garvey set for himself far exceeded his personal abilities and those of his officers. He was a man born out of time. Arrayed against him were the European colonial powers, the American government and the Black Establishment with its white allies. Despite Garvey's success in enrolling millions in this movement, Negroes did not want to live in Africa, and the Africans, who were themselves subdued by the insidious philosophies of colonialism, were not anxious to welcome them there. But the crucial point is that the American Negro considered his heritage and his destiny to be no less American than that of any American white man. They wanted to live in the land for which they had toiled, fought and died. Marcus Garvey's greatest contribution to those who followed him was a new sense of self-esteem, however tentative. Never before Garvey, since Negroes had been free in America, did they dare examine the possibility of accepting themselves and their antecedents at face value. It is true that the limited success of Garveyism was to large degree an emotional reaction against the racial atrocities which swept America following World War I. But it is no less true that he planted the seed for the *mood ebony* through which contemporary Negroes express their disdain for what to them is the delusive ideal of whiteness.

In the 1920's and 1930's the "Negro Renaissance" rediscovered African culture, and Negro art and literature began to explore African themes. But the "talented tenth" (as the Negro intellectuals called themselves), were not *identifying* with blackness. They were simply willing to discuss it in a detached, disinterested way. Only since the emergence of self-governing African states have the Negro intellectuals felt secure enough to risk some degree of identification.

The *mood ebony* is not so much an identification with Africa as it is the abatement of the yearning after whiteness in America, and the rejection of the traditional order of values which, because they cannot be attained with reasonable effort, are productive of increasing anxiety and frustration. It expresses itself as a rejection of integration (sometimes as an insistence on separation). It does not necessarily imply a hatred for the white man, but it does imply a negation of the symbols of his culture, his power and his status. The tendency is, as it was expressed by a Harlem minister, to "let the white man go *his* way— but get him out of *my* way —and fast." But then it is easy to hate what you negate. The Negro has had a long and painful experience of that fact.

The best-known exponents of the *mood ebony* are the Black Muslims of Elijah Muhammad, the inevitable heirs of the Garvey movement. Muhammad does not view his movement as being either "social" or "racial," but as a religion. "My work," he insists, "is divine. And this is what distinguishes it from all other attempts to set the black man in the place Allah has willed him to be." We need not argue the "divine" nature of his mission to be moved to admit that the Muslim Messenger has been an important force in pushing the Negro masses toward a sense of adequacy. The preoccupation of the Black Muslim with his personal and racial image is well known, as is his firm belief that his history and his destiny transcend this brief moment of power which the white man has abused so badly. "We can afford to wait," says Muhammad. "We were here long before the blue-eyed devils were brought to civilization; we will be here for countless generations after they are gone."

Muhammad's avowed millenarianism can be deceptive if it is thought to be generally representative of the Negro masses. *They* cannot wait. They *won't* wait. It has come suddenly to the Negro that if he is going to be saved, he is going to have to save himself. For a hundred years he looked to the heroic institutions of a democratic society to take note of his peculiar condition—a condition not of his making, but one incident to the making of America. For a hundred years his unshakable confidence in The Church, his inalienable confidence in The Law, and his unsophisticated confidence in the social morality of The White Man gave him patience to endure the lash, the rope, the ghetto, the depersonalization of abject discrimination and segregation.[9] Suddenly it was evident that in the mid-twentieth century, here on the threshold of the space age and the precipice of eternity, neither The Church, The Law, nor The White Man had yet effected his release from social bondage and did not seem impressed with an urgency to do so. The whole world was in radical metamorphosis. Undemocratic institutions all over the world were being abandoned. Only in South Africa, Portuguese Angola and the United States did the white man maintain a studied obliviousness to the black man's plea for freedom.

"Work and pray; live on hay. You'll have a pie in the sky when you die." This, the Negro complains bitterly, is his lot. As for the white man's law, many Negroes have come to feel that it was made by white men for the benefit of white men. So they contest it in the streets. One wit has remarked of the law that "Between white men it mediates. Between black men it speculates. And between whites and blacks it deviates." If this were a concept widely held, we would soon be living in chaos.

In the Muslim community the lamp of resentment with its flame of black hatred is carefully tended against the Day of Armageddon—the final confrontation between the forces of good and those of evil, when the non-white races of the world will inundate and (annihilate) the despised whites. Theirs is the hate that hate produced, or so the Black Muslims believe. For if the white man does not hate the black man, then why has he degraded him for so long? "You cannot tell me you love me," says Elijah Muhammad, "when you are giving me hell night and day. If I were to believe that, I would be sicker than you are." The discovery of "the truth about the white man," i.e., his demonic state, his hatred of the Negro, and his perversion of Christianity to support a racist philosophy, is the central fact that makes the Black Muslim movement a popular expression of America's bitterest and most disillusioned Negroes.

The Black Muslims have existed since 1930, but ten years after World War II they suddenly became news. They became news because the ferment in the black ghetto began to produce a rumbling that threatened the racial facade which has so long obscured democracy. The Black Muslims did not produce the rumblings, but they, like the students in the picket lines with bandages on their heads, are the symbols of racial unrest which could explode into a kind of civil violence that would make the infamous Red Summer of 1919 pale by comparison. We are fortunate that instead of civil violence we have had civil disobedience, and although there has been blood, the determined march for civil rights has not yet become bloody.

The Black Muslims are a part of the Negro's all-out struggle for freedom. They represent the extreme radical wing of the Negro's spectrum of protest. But they do not want integration. They want separation. They want no part of anything associated with the white man. The Muslims want a completely separate economy in a separate territory under the hegemony of black men. They want separation because they question the white man's ability to adjust to an integrated society, or even to a pluralistic one. They do not accept nonviolence as an effective principle of negotiation.[10]

The Negro masses have not flocked to join Muhammad's Nation of Islam as they did Marcus Garvey's Universal Negro Improvement Association. Compared to the millions Garvey claimed, Muhammad's seventy or eighty mosques scattered about the country are not numerically impressive. Times have changed. Perhaps Garvey's defeat and deportation is still too vivid in the mind of the race. More likely is the resistance of the contemporary Negro to the idea of "going anywhere," for any reason. He does not want a separate state. The thought of emigrating to Africa seems ridiculous to him. *He is going to stay in America and still be black without apology for his blackness!* There is new pride in being black, and it is this aspect of Muslim philosophy that is impressive far beyond the numbers of men and women who confess the faith that is Elijah Muhammad's interpretation of Islam. And this, not the number of his followers, is the power of the Muslim leader. His black-suited followers, with their exaggerated formality yet a certain sureness, do not defer to the white man. They are polite to everybody.

but they do not defer. And yet they came, for the most part, from the class which survives on deference. The Muslims appear to thrive. Their houses are neat and clean. Their children are not delinquents. They are seldom before the white man's courts except when in contest with the white man himself. Their own explanation is "knowledge"—knowledge about themselves and knowledge of "the truth about the white man." The Negro masses are impressed, and they accept Muhammad's "truth" without necessarily accepting his hatred. There is no compelling drive for integration among the masses; but there is a compulsion to be free—to be free in spite of being black.

If Elijah Muhammad is its Messenger, then James Baldwin, whether or not he accepts the role, is the uncontested philosopher for the *mood ebony*, and Malcolm X is its chief political spokesman. Among them, these three men have an interesting potential for assuming the leadership of America's black masses. Despite his intellectualism, Baldwin does not write for or about intellectuals. His descriptions and his message are visceral, and the images he conjures are the realities which are universal in the black man's experience. Baldwin says of Malcolm X:

> When Malcolm talks or one of the Muslims talks, they articulate for all the Negro people who hear them; who listen to them. They articulate their suffering, the suffering which has been in this country so long denied. That's Malcolm's great authority over his audiences. He corroborates their reality; he tells them that they really exist.[11]

Baldwin could well have been speaking of himself. Certainly he lacks Malcolm's vindictiveness (or, if he has it, its presence is carefully muted by the engaging language through which he communicates himself). And Baldwin, like Malcolm, has a cultivated honesty which can be quite literally disarming.

New York City abounds with black nationalist cults, but with no unified program to promote together the philosophies they separately espouse. In addition to the Black Muslims, there are the Muslim Brotherhood; the United African Nationalist Movement; the Universal African Nationalist Movement; the Cultural Association for Women of African Heritage; The World Federation of African People, Inc.; the Yoruba Temple of New Oyo, and perhaps two dozen others of greater or lesser importance.[12] The *mood ebony* is not black nationalism with an African orientation as is true of most organized nationalist groups. As one Negro businessman put it, it is not so much a desire to identify with Africa as it is a determination to enjoy ham hocks and turnip greens here in America without caring whether or not the white man is watching, and not giving a damn if he is.

Chapter 4

MOOD EBONY:
The Meaning of Malcolm X

And in the silent night
When doors are shut and men are equal
I sought the Lord . . .
Almighty God.

God did not answer
God hid His face.[1]

It was a rare fall day in Chicago. It was the kind of
Saturday morning when one wishes he were on the lakefront
watching the weekend skippers ready their slim craft for a
day of sailing. I decided to walk the nine or ten blocks from
the University of Chicago quadrangle to the blue-trimmed
mansion at 4847 Woodlawn. I did not know any of the students I met along the way. (Old Grads like me are always
peering hopefully here and there as if they really expected
to see someone they used to know—some miracle of reincar-
nation.) Even the old professors die off. Or maybe by progressive moltings they achieve some academic nirvana. Any-
way, the new ones who take their places don't look like the
ones who used to be there. But there is consolation in the
fact that at least the good grey gothic does not change. It is
reassuring to know that there underneath the ivy the granite
is the same.

Pretentiousness is a word ordinarily associated with mansions. If a mansion is not pretentious it may as well be called a house. I had walked past the nineteen-room house on Woodlawn before I realized I was even near it. Somehow, it seemed to escape pretentiousness and I had passed it without really seeing it. Perhaps I was lost in my silent soliloquy on gothic and Old Grads. Perhaps it was because there are many mansions on this quiet street. Their original owners have fled. The always-threatening, hovering advance guard of the stifled *black ghetto* had moved in long ago and settled down in decorous serenity. North, west, and south of the great university the *ghetto* crowds in upon the famous Midway where the university co-eds sun themselves to sleep while reading Aristotle and James Joyce.

I had passed the address I was seeking, but even as I did so the awareness of my oversight was signaled into my consciousness. It was the blue and white trim on the multi-gabled old house—so inconsonant with the studied dignity of the neighboring houses—that halted me and sent me retracing my steps to the concrete driveway I had passed without seeing a moment before.

The number on the gate was 4847. It was the residence of Elijah Muhammad, Messenger to the mystical Nation of Islam in the Wilderness of North America; Prophet to a confident empire of militant Black Muslims who may bow toward Mecca in prayer, but whose every other genuflection is toward Chicago.

The Messenger's house sits rather near the street, and entrance is by way of a portico extending out over the narrow driveway. There was no sign of life anywhere about the grounds as I mounted the concrete steps and rang the bell. Presently the heavy door swung inward and a woman in a white uniform confronted me.

"Yes?"

"I have an appointment with Mr. Muhammad." I gave her my card.

"Yes," she said again. The interrogative was spent. There was no emotional content in her voice whatever. "The Messenger is expecting you." I followed the woman into a small foyer and waited for her to tell Muhammad that I had come.

I had been there before. Once during my early research on the Black Muslim movement I had had dinner with the Prophet and had spent the entire evening listening to his explication of Black Islam as he had learned it from Wali Fard in the 1930's. A year or so later, in another marathon session, I had filled a small notebook with data on the Messenger's interpretation of history, the respective roles proper to Black Men and white men in social and political relations, and the eschatological promise inherent in the manifest destiny of the Black Nation he hoped to unite under the Star and Crescent. I remembered that there had been a comparative quality of cogency to these heterodox arguments that never seemed to come through in the addresses I had heard Muhammad deliver in the various Muslim temples about the country.

I awaited the Prophet's appearance with some apprehension. The book I had written about his movement displeased some of his ministers very greatly, and they had not been reticent about their displeasure. A delegation of the faithful had called on me in Atlanta "to discuss the book," and Atlanta minister Jeremiah X expressed the desire to burn the books as fast as they came off the press. Too, I had received some uncomplimentary letters, one or two of which were thick enough to require my paying extra postage in order to get at the insults inside.

That some of the faithful would be unhappy about my treatment of the movement and certain of its leaders was not unexpected. Since the Black Muslims (like most of the religiously devout) themselves offer no pretensions about objectivity, it would be naive to expect them to be clamorous in their applause over an objective analysis of their doctrines or activities. Nor was it altogether surprising that some of the protesting letters came from people who said they were not Muslims, but who, because they do not like white people, read the book with myopic impairments.

As I waited in the little foyer, I could sense Muhammad's approach even though the sound of his footsteps was stillborn in the thick grey carpeting. Suddenly he was in the room—an electric sort of presence—and I was trying to assess the confusion I felt at what seemed an intuitive response to it.

"Welcome, Professor!" The Muslim leader held out a lean brown hand as if to underscore his greeting. I offered my hand in return while searching his face for some clue as to whether the reception was perfunctory. There was no clue. His eyes were steady and his handshake was firm. He did not smile, but then I could not remember having ever seen Muhammad smile. If in fact he does smile on occasion, that is not the image by which he is remembered.

I followed the Muslim leader into a large dining room where two young Muslims were seated facing each other near one end of the table. They arose at the approach of the Messenger and remained standing until he had taken his seat at the head of the table. I knew them both: John X, Muhammad's secretary, and James X, Minister of the Chicago Mosque. While they were standing, I greeted each of them in turn:

"Secretary John!"

"As-salaam alaikum!"

"Minister James!"

"As-salaam alaikum!"

We shook hands and sat down.

The Muslims had been drinking coffee and at a signal from Muhammad the woman who had answered the door appeared and placed a cup of the steaming black brew in front of me.

It is Muhammad's custom to teach his ministers in a kind of informal briefing session each Saturday morning. These are not strategy sessions designed to accomplish some immediate, tangible goals (although such conferences are frequent). The Messenger's Saturday morning lectures are inculcatory: their end is the progressive displacement of Christian (i.e., the white man's) values with a neo-Fardian interpretation of Black Islam.

As I joined the circle the Messenger was addressing himself to the natural heritage of the Black Man and the superficiality of the white man's sense of moral responsibility. It is the white man who disturbs the peace of the world, he was saying. "The teachings of the white Christians divide the natural unity of peoples. They have put Asians against Asians, Africans against Africans, brothers against brothers all over the world throughout their civilized history. This is the secret of their power." The congenital blindness of the Negro in America is demonstrated in his expectation that the white man will ever give him justice, he said.

"The white man is incapable of justice except to his own kind. *By nature he is incapable. By nature he is a devil!* In trusting him we close our eyes to knowledge. In loving him we ally ourselves with evil. The white man is incapable of loving anyone who is not white. It is time for us to go for self. The white man's rule is ended. The future belongs to the black people of the world. The future is here if we can wake our people who have been doped by the white man's promises to set them free and make them equal!"

I tried momentarily to bare my reason to this potent hypodermic to see if I could get the "lift" I have seen transport thousands in the Muslim mosques in the *black ghettos* of America.

Across the damask-covered table in an immaculate grey suit and a powder-blue bow tie, Secretary John X was writing. I could not see his eyes for he did not look up, but I knew that he had missed no word uttered by his master. I had been told that John had a college degree, and I thought how incongruous seemed his role of amanuensis to the semi-literate Messenger of Allah. "John X, the black Baruch," I said to myself. And at that very moment, as if he too were thinking of another prophet and another scribe 2,800 years before, Muhammad was pronouncing doom for all the enemies of Black Islam. Jeremiah to proclaim—Baruch to write it down! Elijah Muhammad—Secretary John!

And now his remarks were addressed to me: "You intellectual people should pay good attention—the white man wants to call you by your slave name. Now those who refuse to give up the mark of the beast must die with the beast! The white devils want to set you against your own people, but they will murder you if you forget that you are black! Give up the white man's name. Learn to love your own people."

I shuddered a little. I had always thought my own name euphonious. Suppose (I gave myself a private challenge), following the Black Muslim custom of discarding "European" surnames—"badges of slavery" the Muslims call them —I had to be known as "Eric X" the rest of my life! And my son would be "Eric 2X." And my wife and daughter would become mere cross marks on my income tax returns. So many X's could be confusing!

On the same side of the table with myself Minister James sat enraptured. He was seated nearest Muhammad but his whole body was tense as he strained to capture and memorize every word that fell from the Prophet's lips. Occasionally he uttered an ejaculation: "That's right!" but the fixed smile never left his face. His whole posture was one of unrelieved expectancy. I thought about the old, old lady with the gruff voice who used to sit on the edge of the front pew and "talk back" to the preacher in the revival meetings when I was a kid in Alabama a long time ago.

Raymond Sharrieff came in. Muhammad paused while we exchanged greetings. Sharrieff is Muhammad's son-in-law. He is also Supreme Captain of the FOI, i.e., the Fruit of Islam, the secret protective arm of the Muslim Movement. Sharrieff sat down next to John, directly across the table from myself. The woman brought more coffee and the Messenger resumed his teaching.

"If the average black preacher would study the history of Christianity he wouldn't believe in it or teach it to his people. The white man will not call you 'brother.' There is

no brotherhood in his religion." Muhammad then went on
to tell about his experiences in the Holy City of Mecca and
in the other Islamic lands where he has traveled. "It is a beautiful and touching thing to get among your own people and
see the love that exists. The white man cannot love you. *By
nature he cannot love you!* But you must love each other and
protect your own kind. The white man will take care of
himself!"

The chimes sounded and the woman who had brought
the coffee went to answer the door. A moment later Malcolm
X strode into the room. Every Muslim came to his feet to
greet the tall minister from New York's Mosque No. 7.
Muhammad embraced him in Muslim fashion, kissing him
gently on each cheek.

"As-salaam Alaikum!"

"Wah alaikum salaam!"

"As-salaam Alaikum!"

"Wah alaikum salaam!"

Each of the brothers greeted the smiling Malcolm—but
Muhammad would hardly let him go. "How is the baby?"
the Prophet asked, referring to Malcolm's infant daughter
(who interestingly enough is named for Attila the Hun).
"When did you leave New York?" There was genuine
affection here between these two, not unlike the affection
between a father and son who has done well for the family
name. One could sense that the little drama being acted here
was real, for the chief actors were for a time completely
oblivious of all others who were in the room. I had never
doubted Malcolm's absolute loyalty to Muhammad, but now
I made a mental note: Muhammad had never doubted it
either. There was a broad grin on his face as he waved Mal-

colm to a seat at the long table. It was the first time I had ever seen Muhammad smile.

The teaching resumed: but now *two* were writing, for the ubiquitous Malcolm X would be quoting his master in a half-dozen cities within as many days. "Mr. Muhammad teaches us . . ."

"We can't make a future for twenty million black people by lying around the employment office. We have to go for self! . . . We forget overnight what the white man did to us . . ." Mr. Muhammad was speaking.[2]

Early the next morning a bomb was to explode in a Negro Church in Birmingham, Alabama, where the right of black citizens to enjoy the fruits of democracy was being contested in blood and invective. Four little Negro girls, guilty of no crime worse than trying to worship the God the white man taught them to love and believe in, would be murdered. By Monday morning there would be more Black Muslims and fewer Negro Christians in America.

A few months later Malcolm X was suspended from the Black Muslim organization. The reason made public for his suspension was "insubordination." Against the express command of Muhammad to "keep quiet" on the matter of the tragic death of President Kennedy, Malcolm X made a public statement to the effect that "the Kennedy chickens had finally come home to roost." The gross indelicacy of such a remark was offensive to millions of Americans irrespective of color or political party. But published reports provide an interesting footnote to history in that in at least two white schools in Alabama and Georgia, the news of the President's assassination was received with cheers and rejoicing, and in Texas a white college student spoke candidly of his pleasure that Kennedy was dead. President Kennedy was not loved universally. Great men seldom are, and his murder is incontrovertible evidence that there were some who did not wish him well. It is to the credit of the American sense of propriety that at his death so few anti-Kennedy remarks were given currency in the press. When Franklin Roosevelt died in 1945, I can remember a series of fights between Negroes and whites at the naval base where I was stationed over conflicting emotions about "the Great White Father," as he was referred to by those who hated him.

The point at issue, however, is whether Malcolm X was suspended and subsequently withdrew from the Black Muslim movement over his vulgarity regarding President Kennedy. The short answer is "no." The whole public career of Malcolm X is studded with intemperate remarks and there is no indication that the Muslim hierarchy ever considered them with other than approbation. On June 3, 1962, for example, Malcolm interrupted an address before some 1500 Negroes in a Los Angeles church to give thanks to Allah that "he dropped an airplane out of the sky with 120 white people on it." To Malcolm, this was "a very beautiful thing," and for such a blessing he promised Allah (God) that "we will continue to pray, and we hope that every day another plane falls out of the sky. We call on our God," he said happily, and "He gets rid of 120 of them at one whop."[3] For these sentiments he was cheered by the Muslims present, and there is no evidence that they incurred the displeasure of any Muslim official. Further, the public statements of Elijah Muhammad himself—who is referred to by the Muslim newspaper *Muhammad Speaks* as "the most fearless Black Man in

America"—have seldom been models of moderation. In fact, a significant aspect of the Muslims' appeal has always been their openly expressed hostility toward the white man, for in listening to the Muslim ministers castigate their oppressors, the millions of Negroes most accommodated to the status quo may share vicariously in a glorious moment of aggression.

The facts are that the Messenger and his black Machiavelli came suddenly (and logically) upon a parting of the ways without either having consciously contemplated such a possibility. Muhammad had rescued Malcolm from prison and from a life of sordidness and crime, and had guided him to international prominence as a spokesman for the Black Man. In return, Malcolm had given Muhammad an absolute loyalty that was fanatical in its intensity. Not even in his most unguarded moments did Malcolm ever permit himself to forget that Muhammad was in fact his savior.

It is clear that Muhammad had no more intention of dropping Malcolm than Malcolm had of cutting himself loose. Internal jealousy and envy played an important part in the rupture. As Muhammad's health grew poorer, he began to spend more and more time in seclusion at his mansion in Phoenix, Arizona, and Malcolm became acknowledged universally *outside* the movement as chief spokesman for the Black Muslims. His face was well known on the television screens and university campuses across the country. Inside the movement the word trickled up to Muhammad—and then became insistent: "Brother Malcolm is overshadowing the Messenger. Brother Malcolm must be curbed!" At first Muhammad would listen to none of the rumors, but then the press began to speculate on the real locus of power in the movement, and upon the ailing Muhammad's successor. Something had to be done.

Contrary to public opinion, Malcolm X was never in the power structure of the Muslim movement. This did not mean that he would not have been a logical (and powerful) contender for leadership in the event of Muhammad's death, for during the ten or more years he served Muhammad, he organized nearly all the mosques that came into being during that period. But the established power has always been in the hands of Muhammad himself; his son-in-law, Raymond Sharrieff (who heads the secret para-military order, the Fruit of Islam); and other members of the family. Malcolm was relieved of his post as editor of *Muhammad Speaks* and its offices were moved from New York to Muslim headquarters in Chicago. A bit later he was relieved of his duties at the important Washington, D.C., mosque where he had been filling in since the ousting of Lucius X, and replaced with Lonnie X (Ph.D.), a brilliant young mathematician formerly of Atlanta University. Then came the Kennedy affair.

By now the handwriting was clear; both Malcolm and Muhammad began reassessment. For the first time Malcolm permitted himself an act of open defiance to the will of Muhammad. On three separate occasions Muhammad warned Malcolm to keep quiet about the death of President Kennedy. In the end Malcolm spoke out in an act of deliberate insubordination. The issue was not one of hatred for Mr. Kennedy (except insofar as he belonged to a hated class). At issue was a contest of wills and the decision to commit an act that could only set the stage for schism. Malcolm knew this, of course, and having made his defiance he was forthwith suspended. A good part of his period of suspension was spent in Miami indoctrinating his Muslim brother Cassius Clay with the idea that his forthcoming fight with Sonny Listen symbolized a fight to the death between Catholicism (a "white religion") and Islam ("the religion of the Black Man"), and that it was the will of Allah that Clay should vanquish Liston, who was pictured as a pawn in the hands of the white devils. Once Allah had been vindicated Malcolm X returned to New York to announce his break with Muhammad and his Black Muslims.

On the morning of March 12, 1964, Malcolm X called a press conference at the Park Sheraton Hotel in New York City to announce his break with Muhammad and his plans to organize his own movement, the Muslim Mosque, Incorporated. The primary purpose of the press conference, he said, was to clarify his position in the struggle for human rights, especially with regard to politics and nonviolence. His prepared speech began with a reaffirmation of faith in Islam, and in the wisdom of Elijah Muhammad. "I am and always will be a Muslim," he declared. "I still believe that Mr. Muhammad's analysis of the [race] problem is the most realistic, and that his solution is the best one. This means that I too believe the best solution is complete separation, with our people going back home, to our African homeland." Having dispensed with these gratuities, the "Big X" moved swiftly to the heart of the matter:

> But separation back to Africa is still a long range program, and while it is yet to materialize, twenty-two million of our people who are still here in America need better food, clothing, housing, education and jobs *right now* [Italics his] ....
>
> Our political philosophy will be Black Nationalism. Our

cultural emphasis will be Black Nationalism . . . the Muslim
Mosque, Inc. will be organized in such a manner as to provide for the active participation of all Negroes in our political, economic, and social programs, despite their religious
or non-religious beliefs.

The olive branch was extended to Negro civil rights
leaders:

> I'm not out to fight other Negro leaders or organizations.
> We must find a common approach, a common solution to a
> common problem. As of this minute, I've forgotten every-
> thing bad the other leaders have said about me, and I pray
> they can also forget the many bad things I've said about
> them . . . We must stop worrying about the threat that we
> seem to think we pose to each other's personal prestige, and
> concentrate our united efforts toward solving the unending
> hurt that is being done daily to our people here in America.

He interpreted the political philosophy of Black Nationalism to mean that "We must control the politics and the
politicians of our community. They must no longer take
orders from outside forces. We will organize and sweep out
of office all Negro politicians who are puppets for the outside forces."

There was an urgent appeal to youth:

> Our accent will be on youth: We need new ideas, new
> methods, new approaches. We will call upon young stu-
> dents of political science throughout the nation to help us
> . . . We are completely disenchanted with the old, adult,
> established politicians. We want to see some new faces . . .
> more militant faces . . . Whites can help us [financially]
> but they can't join us. There can be no black-white unity
> until there is first some black unity.

Malcolm closed his short speech with what has been widely interpreted as a call for the Negro masses to arm themselves, and a veiled threat of violence. Said he:

> It is criminal to teach a man not to defend himself when he is the constant victim of brutal attacks. It is legal and lawful to own a shotgun or a rifle. We believe in obeying the law. In areas where our people are the constant victims of brutality, and the government seems unwilling or unable to protect them, . . . we should form rifle clubs that can be used to defend our lives and our property in time of emergency such as happened last year in Birmingham, Plaquemine, La.; Cambridge, Md. and Danville, Va. When our people are bitten by dogs, they are within their rights to kill those dogs.

> We should be peaceful, law-abiding . . . but the time has come for the American Negro to fight back in self defense whenever and wherever he is being unjustly attacked. If the government thinks I am wrong for saying this, then let the government start doing its job.[4]

It was to be expected that the accepted civil rights leaders continued to maintain a wary distance from Malcolm X despite his overtures for "unity." There was, too, some apprehension in the press over the prospect of Negro "rifle-clubs" being introduced into the midst of a tense racial situation. Some Negro leaders sought to reassure the disturbed white press by ridiculing the idea and denouncing the Muslim leader for introducing it. To many Negro leaders this was proof positive of Malcolm's irresponsibility within or without the Black Muslim movement, and of his danger to a civil rights movement committed to litigation and non-violence.

Malcolm's rifle-club statement would have probably caused much less concern except for the fact that the recent murder of President Kennedy had made America acutely conscious of the easy availability of firearms and their potential danger in the hands of the irresponsible. Too, it is common knowledge among Negro leaders and law officials that Negroes in the South (like whites) have been steadily buying guns for a decade. Certainly Negroes have no aggressive intentions as it seems to be feared, but for most Negroes "a gun in the house" is a matter of protection for home and family. It is clear from a scattering of incidents across the South in recent years that the day in which Negroes will accept intimidation in their own homes is very nearly past. Negroes remember too (and talk about the fact) that the race riots in Chicago and Detroit a generation ago were stopped, not by the police and the militia, but only when the Negro victims armed themselves and fought back. Another factor in the rifle-club matter is the sense of collective guilt felt by the responsible Southerners. Negroes have been beaten, bombed, shot and mutilated almost at will in some parts of the South for as long as there have been Negroes there. Neither the local or federal officials have been able or willing to afford them protection. In such a situation, the white Southerner knows what *he* would do.

On the other hand, it would be rash to underestimate the intentions or the capacities of Malcolm X. Malcolm has had a long and arduous training in the philosophy of Black Islam, which, while presenting itself as a religion of peace, is publicly committed to the *lex talionis* ("an eye for an eye and a tooth for a tooth)." "We teach our people," said Malcolm when he was Muhammad's chief lieutenant, "never to be the aggressor. Never to look for trouble. But if any man molests you, *may Allah bless you!*" The numerous instances in which they have been involved in overt strife in the penitentiaries, on the streets and even in the courtrooms of America give ample evidence of the seriousness with which the Black Muslims apply this maxim to their everyday affairs.[5]

Malcolm X appears on the threshold of black leadership at a very crucial moment in the history of the racial struggle in America. Thanks to more sober Negro leadership and its white allies, the bastions of segregation have been steadily reduced now for a decade or more. There is some school desegregation; employment opportunities have improved. It is no longer strange to see a Negro face in a television commercial. In parts of the South Negroes may eat where they please, play golf on the municipal courses, and in some cases worship with their fellow-Christians who may be white. Congress has passed a new Civil Rights bill. But poverty and ignorance remain. And discrimination and prejudice are far from being disestablished. There is anger, resentment, frustration and hatred.

There is a certain anxiety pervading the white and Negro communities in the South and in the North. The white man feels that he has given up something that was uniquely his. Perhaps he has given up too much? And yet the blacks are not satisfied. They push. *They continue to push!* For their part the Negroes know that what the white man has given up so grudgingly and with such fabian gradualness was not the white man's to withhold or bestow. What the white man has kept pocketed so long was the life blood of a subject people, that without which they could neither be free nor whole. There is still a great distance to go, and it is this distance rather than that already traveled that creates the anxiety.

What will be the role of Malcolm X in the crucial period ahead? Some observers, such as George Daniels, a widely read Negro writer and a careful student of the Harlem scene, accept Malcolm's break with Muhammad at face value and see no future for him outside the Muslim movement. Writing in the April issue of *News Illustrated*, Daniels argues:

> To save face Malcolm X had to announce his own departure from the Black Muslim movement and make it appear as a political and philosophical split . . .

> Malcolm X's future is now based upon aligning himself with Cassius Clay for monetary and popularity purposes, and establishing radical differences between his movement and that of Elijah Muhammad . . . for publicity purposes he will tend to create disturbances and remain a controversial figure. His program now is one of desperation; a drowning man grasping for the proverbial straw he thinks could save his life.

At the superficial level Mr. Daniels' analysis is undoubtedly a good one. But the matter is deeper than appears on the surface. Malcolm's break with Muhammad was a deliberate act in the face of well-considered consequences, an act thought out carefully over the period of the three months during which he was suspended. At any time, Malcolm could have returned to the fold, even after public announcement of his departure. Discussing the matter in the elegant silence of Mr. Muhammad's Phoenix retreat, I asked whether Malcolm could return to the movement if he chose. Muhammad's answer was that "entire submission is always acceptable." To Muhammad it was a question of who should lead and who should follow. "If you are my leader," he said with some evidence of rancor, "I will follow your teachings. I don't tell my people to commit suicide by telling them to arm. Fight against those who fight against you—yes. But this does not always mean fighting with weapons. Moses did not conquer the Egyptians with weapons. Mine is a divine work. It must proceed according to what is divine."

Turning again to Malcolm he said, "I warned him just an hour before his lecture to keep his mouth shut. We are all under the government and should show respect. When I suspended him, Malcolm took it for an insult to be set down for any length of time. He was too proud. A man seeking exaltation sometimes goes to extremes."

Clearly Malcolm X and Elijah Muhammad had reached a point of ideological divergence. Age and health are key ideological conditioners. Since 1960 the Muhammad has tended more and more toward retirement. His strident attacks on the "blue-eyed devils" have all but ceased, and the Messenger is almost wistfully concerned with the "divine" nature of his work. This, now, is his insistent message. The Muslims have fared well under Muhammad's leadership. There are no new temples, but the membership is faithful in its tithing and the businesses of the movement seem to thrive. An efficient staff in Chicago runs the newspaper and carries on the day-to-day business of the movement. Being a Black Muslim is respectable as far as the Negro masses are concerned. Whatever else their differences, a shift toward conservatism in the mood of the Muslim movement left no place for Malcolm X. Malcolm X is a revolutionary by nature, and as such there was no longer any place for him in the Black Muslim movement.

In his calculated break with Muhammad, what then does Malcolm X see as his role in the Negro's struggle for freedom? He has stated publicly time and time again that passivism and nonviolence are not effective means of gaining the white man's respect or of securing the Negro his freedom. Nor does he seem psychologically prepared to wait for the Armageddon Muhammad has promised the Black Muslims. In a long interview following his decision to go it alone, Malcolm admitted that the two most important events in his life were his decision to follow Muhammad and his decision to leave Muhammad.

It is significant that among Malcolm's first acts as a leader in his own right was a visit to Mecca and a long tour of black Africa. The first act effected and confirmed his status as an orthodox Muslim, and he became in consequence thereof El Haji Malik El Shabazz (the prefix El Haji signifying his pilgrimage to the Holy City). The objectives of the second act may only be speculated upon. But his journey was certainly not that of a mere tourist, for Malcolm's contacts in the Afro-Asian world are many. Before he left New York he had secured letters of introduction to the heads of state or people in government of at least a half-dozen Afro-Asian states, and his advisors had prepared for him a detailed itinerary with political briefings on each person he was to see. A communication from Beirut carried the following message:

> Am speaking at the American University of Beirut this evening, sponsored by the African students. This is a beautiful city reflecting the best of the East and the West.
> *El Haji Malik El Shabazz*

Another from Saudi Arabia said:

Allah has blessed me to be the State Guest of His Excellency Prince Feisal. I have made my Pilgrimage to Mecca, and will visit Medina in a few days, Allah willing. Never have I witnessed such *hospitality* and *brotherhood* as is practical here in this Ancient Holy Land the home of Abraham [Italics his].

El Haji Malik El Shabazz

Yet another from Casablanca:

My journey is almost ended and I have a much broader scope than when I started out five weeks ago, which I believe will add new life and dimension to our people's struggle for freedom and human dignity.

El Haji Malik El Shabazz

Back home again he was confronted with the problem of rounding out a philosophy and translating into action what he had toured Africa and Asia to see and to hear.

The black revolution in this country is not a specter that was created yesterday by a cabal of Negroes who suddenly decided to reverse the social order and fight for Negro rights. The roots of the revolution are deep in the soul of the race and in the history of America. The revolution began when the first slave landed at Jamestown and it has been continuing ever since. Individuals and organizations, now one, now another, have carried the fight for almost four hundred years—the NAACP alone for more than a half-century. But never before has the revolution reached such proportions that it has become the center of our national concern. At any given moment the fight is universal throughout America—from St. Augustine to San Francisco; from Los

Angeles to Boston. But despite the universality of the revolution the total Negro community has yet to commit itself to an active involvement. The psychological involvement has been, for some time now, total or nearly so. But the dynamics of involvement have been restricted to a relative handful of Negroes—probably less than 1 percent of the Negro population—and their white supporters. The Negro masses have not been involved, but they are ready for involvement. It is the knowledge of this reality that motivates Malcolm X and makes him potentially the most powerful and perhaps the most dangerous Negro in America. A man of extraordinary gifts with a diabolical appeal to the sense of injury and the sense of pride of the disinherited, Malcolm X is himself the Man on the Black Horse who stalks in the wings as the tortured masses come awake to the possibilities of freedom, or foredoom themselves to increased frustration through some chauvinistic enterprise.

Despite the reassurances of "nice people," hatred is deep in the black ghetto, and the feeling is common among Negroes and whites who are involved in the struggle that America will either solve its racial problem soon, or be destroyed by it. The Reverend Milton Galamison of New York, who has been identified as a black radical, is one who agrees that "if the race problem is not solved, this country will surely perish," for, says Galamison, "I do not believe that it is imperative that this country survive . . ."[6] But so careful and (relatively) conservative a leader as Dr. John Morsell, Assistant to the Executive Secretary of the NAACP, is even more emphatic:

> One thing is clear and unequivocal: our survival as a viable democracy is dependent upon a successful outcome of this

revolution. To weigh the chances of its success is therefore no more and no less than to weigh the chances of the United States of America. My own feeling is that there is at best a fifty percent possibility that we will overcome the dangerous trends and tendencies which militate against success.[7]

Morsell, like other more objective leaders, is acutely conscious of the direction the black revolution could take. There is no need to cry "wolf," but Negroes and whites alike who do not wish to see this country become racially polarized will be constantly alert to that possibility. Whereas a scant four years ago the NAACP was willing to dismiss the Black Muslim movement as "a creature of the press," Dr. Morsell now sees it as an example of the extremity to which Negroes may be driven—or led under the press of continued social anxiety:

> Negroes continue . . . to tread a rather narrow path between faith and frustration; they have not yet enjoyed enough progress to be entirely reassured as to what the American democracy can do to rescue them. The Black Muslims are an illustration of where some go when they decide it can do nothing, and more will go with them if progress is not constant and repaid. *Retaliatory violence is not too far in the wings either—if indeed it is in the wings at all* [Italics mine].[8]

Malcolm X says that he will prove that the black man cannot get civil rights in this country. He says further that "The black man is maturing . . . waking up. That is why I say we will have real violence. I have found out that the black man in the street thinks like I think."[9] The irony of the matter is that Malcolm's thesis will be ridiculously easy to prove for sometime to come. Almost no Negroes in America believe in the present availability of their civil rights. Even before the Civil Rights bill of 1964 was signed, major Negro leadership as represented by Martin Luther King, Jr., and Roy Wilkins was engaged in a public debate over how soon Negroes should test for compliance. Certainly it is true that if the bill is not implemented it will add immeasurably to the frustrations of the Negro masses who never believed that it would be implemented in the first place. All during the long debate over the bill, Negroes were generally unimpressed, and their low-keyed interest was particularly exasperating for some politicians who were making a determined effort to appear "liberal" in an election year. Some Negro leaders publicly belittled the importance of the bill, thereby exciting the ire of the NAACP's Roy Wilkins, who has the intelligence to understand the persuasive power of law in effecting social change.

The significance of Malcolm X has little to do with Malcolm X as a person. For almost a decade now, America has listened with apprehension and ridicule, and shame and catharsis and fear and approbation to the brutal message of black hatred it has been Malcolm's self-chosen destiny to deliver. Malcolm is important only to the degree that he is right in his assumption that "the black man in the street thinks the way [Malcolm X] thinks." Even if this were so, Malcolm is at this point the symbol rather than the leader of an important new dimension of the black revolution. As a consequence, many of the questions being asked about him as a person have no meaning: "Why did he leave Muhammad?" "Will he be assassinated by Muhammad's followers?" Will his newfound orthodoxy qualify his intense racism?"

No matter. His leaving Muhammad is ultimately important only to Muhammad. His assassination, should such misfortune befall him, would have little impact outside black nationalist circles unless his assassin happened to be white—in which case it would be difficult to estimate the carnage. As for his newfound religiously inspired and highly qualified acceptance of some whites, I can only recall Malcolm's own statements that "a leopard does not change his spots in or out of the jungle," and "a cat can have kittens in an oven, but that doesn't make them biscuits." In short, there seems to be little reason to believe that he has "changed," or that he thinks the white man has.

Malcolm X is a symbol—a symbol of the increasing irritability of the Negro lower class. He is the symbol of the uninvolved leaderless masses whose hatred for the white man has been most often expressed as self-hatred, and whose vast potential for aggression has been displaced upon each other. By 1970 there will be twenty-five million Negroes in the United States. By 1980 there will be thirty-three million. This is a formidable minority within any population, no matter how large.

This is an age of anxiety for all subject peoples. Negroes in America are extremely concerned lest they go down in history as civilization's cruelest paradox—the most culturally advanced subject peoples of modern times, who are citizens of the world's greatest democracy, but who, for all that, are unable to free themselves. Here in America the process of restoring to the Negro the fundamental rights of human beings has been going on for a hundred years, and the end is nowhere in sight. In no other aspect of our national life have we moved so slowly and in such bad grace. As a consequence we have created and we perpetuate a most excruciating anxiety which colors all our intergroup and interpersonal relations.

The psychologists tell us that "anxiety is the subjective experience of the organism in a catastrophic condition"; that it is "the apprehension of the disapproval of significant persons in one's interpersonal world." Anxiety derives too, as every American Negro knows, from the persistent efforts of the individual to acquire success and prestige in the face of the formidable social, economic and political taboos which qualify his existence in America. Success and social esteem represent the dominant values of our culture, and the successful competition for these values provides the individual with purpose and self-validation. Failure results in the loss of self-esteem and establishes deep feelings of inferiority. In a segregated, prejudiced, race-conscious society such as ours, the Negro's attainment of these values is precluded, or so beset with obstacles as to be considered precluded.

Social anxiety develops in proportion to the threat to the individual's opportunities for self-validation and social esteem, i.e., validation in the eyes of others. These are values essential to existence as a whole personality, values without which the meaning and purpose in life are seriously eroded. It is only in recent times that the mass Negro, *the most accommodated Negro*, has come to the realization that his life could be better than it is, that there is a reason, a cause—*a remediable cause*—for the peculiar circumstances of his lot. He has caught a glimpse of freedom—in Africa, in Asia, in America. He will never again be the same and, depending on the nature of his leadership, he will count his long years of accommodation as license.

This is the meaning of Malcolm X. He is the raw, un-refined symbol of the awakening, a microcosm of the intense emotions and social aberrancy which characterize the *black ghetto* and which remain, even yet, invisible to the white man.

Chapter 5

BLACK CHAUVINISM:
The Armageddon Complex

I am alone
Alone I must make my way
Struggle alone
Out of the night to day.[1]

The black revolution in America has not been a "black" revolution at all. It has been a revolution on behalf of black men and women. And black children, that they may some-day lose, not their blackness, but the stigma—the incon-venience of being black in white America. It has not been a black revolution because from John Brown to William Lloyd Garrison, and from John F. Kennedy to Bruce Klunder, the white man, the hated symbol of black oppres-sion, has shared the black man's misery, his hopes, his defeats and his victories. With money, and leadership, and in the ranks, where heads have been bashed and blood has wet the pavements, the Negro revolutionary has had a friend and an ally in the long and bitter fight against tyranny and oppres-sion.

I do not share the sentiments of those who say that the Negro can make no progress without the aid of the white man. If there were *no* white men willing to hazard their lives and their fortunes and their social status for the Negro's civil rights and the moral atonement of our gully-washed democracy, the Negro would still fight for his freedom and ultimately he would win it. But at what cost in blood and sacrifice and how far down the long, grey years of the future? The white allies constitute not only a numerical asset, but a strategic one as well. Moreover, they prevent this struggle from developing a strict racial polarization, and they make the Negro's fight America's fight for self-redemption.

The modern-day Negro has had a taste of honey. He has developed a corps of black leadership, and he has seen freedom. He has seen black men suffer, like Martin Luther King and James Farmer. He has seen black men die, like Medgar Evers. He has seen fortitude in the face of women like Rosa Parks, and determination on the brow of a hundred Daisy Bateses and Gloria Richardsons. And he has seen dignity and restraint mirrored in the faces of black youth at Clinton, Tennessee; Little Rock, Arkansas; Oxford, Mississippi; St. Augustine, Florida. Inevitably has come the cry: "Who needs the white man?"

We do. The Negro needs the white man. He needs him to make his freedom complete and meaningful; to help him forget the horror of the past; to share with him the vision of the future. America needs the white man to search with the Negro for a peace that is lasting and just; to strain out the bitterness and the hatred that could keep this nation divided for centuries.

I have heard the ridicule of the white moderates, who without question have on occasion fumbled when deftness was needed, and who have at other times drawn back from a confrontation with some ultimate test, real or felt by Negroes of militant purpose. There is no excuse for weakness, except that it is an evidence of finitude. But if the black revolution stands to purge itself of all human frailty, it must shortly come to an end.

Much has been made of the "white backlash," the retreat of the white liberals of the North when they have had to confront at home the problems of racial adjustment they fought so vigorously to resolve in the South. It is frightening to find bigotry at home, and it is disillusioning to be deserted when the offensive edges toward the home ground of friends who have fought valiantly in faraway places. What the white man did not realize was that the Negro's offensive is *total*. The limited forays of yesterday for limited objectives in the "pagan" South have been over ever since the NAACP stopped fighting for "separate but equal" and the Supreme Court confirmed that separate cannot be equal—more than a decade ago. Since that time the objectives of the revolution have been unlimited. They lie in the South, but also in the North. They are in education, and voting, and housing, and employment, and public accommodations in distant places and right around home. But the victory sought by the black revolution is a victory for America, one in which the Negro will share incidentally, and one in which every American has a right and a duty to participate.

There is a counter-backlash that is plaguing the civil rights movement. It is a growing insistence that the rights movement is in fact a black revolution, and that the white man has through financial control subverted its leadership and taken over planning and direction. This is manifestly untrue, but the visibility of whites in large numbers in the March on Washington and the voter registration drives in

Mississippi lends credence to the assertion. Further, the support that one or two foundations have given to various civil rights projects has led to the ridiculous allegations that Negro leadership has been "bought out by Jews" or by the white man in general.

All this has led increasingly to a noisy clamor that the black man must go it alone, or that he must seek "black" allies among the Afro-Asian bloc in the United Nations. Elijah Muhammad's dictum, "you can't whip a man when he's helping you," has been resurrected and used to explain everything from the school situation in Chicago to the Hasidic patrols in Brooklyn. All this has been productive of an increasing bitterness and an accompanying return toward the black chauvinism which characterizes the philosophies of Marcus Garvey, Elijah Muhammad and Malcolm X. When Malcolm X contemptuously brushed aside the fact that Bruce Klunder, a white minister, sacrificed his life in Cleveland in the interest of civil rights by announcing that "We're not going to stand up and applaud one white person when twenty-two million American Negroes are being tortured," he was speaking for a multitude of Negroes. In response to Malcolm's outburst, one Negro woman of evident educational attainment wrote to a New York newspaper: "I know that I am expected to flatly denounce Malcolm X's callous reaction to the young minister's death. And I'm almost crying inside because I can't. My first thought was 'How tragic,' but before that thought was cold I was thinking 'But they started it! Years ago after an explosion in the Gary steel mills one of my girl friends told me how her shock . . . changed to relieved *laughter* because only white men were killed . . . when that plane from Atlanta crashed in

Paris it was sensitive little me who said, aloud, 'Good! It serves them right!' "[2]

The fact that the white man "started it all" should not obscure the equally important fact that at least *some* white men are trying to end it. The blanket condemnation of *all* white men makes no more sense than the blanket assumption that *all* Negroes are stupid and inferior. There is obvious evidence to refute either position. And yet the *racial* guilt of the white man is very widely assumed. In the fall of 1963, Dr. Jay T. Wright, a white educator who has spent much of his professional life teaching Negroes in the South (at great personal sacrifice), was vigorously booed when he told an audience at a southern Negro College that he was unwilling "to assume personally a burden of guilt for what some white men did to some Negroes" in the development of American history. In the question-and-answer period following the lecture, some of the student leaders attacked viciously the idea that *any* white man could exempt himself from responsibility for the behavior of the white race in America, and in this argument the students were joined by members of the faculty, who were no less adamant about the corporate guilt of white America.

These attitudes are disturbing at a time when after twenty years we are still trying to assess our feelings about "the German people" and "their" responsibility for the murder of six million Jews. To many Negroes it is a simple matter of black and white. White is evil. "Where in America can you go and be accepted *without reservation* by the white man?" The issue is not as simple as that, of course, for we are all creatures of the culture of which we are a part, and in this culture the *prevailing* sentiment conditioning our values and

ordering our behavior has for whatever reasons—bias, ignorance, fear, economic advantage—not found the Negro
"acceptable." But this is not to say that there exist *no* individuals who have not emancipated themselves from the
prison of prejudice. An insistent phrase from the writings of
Elijah Muhammad haunts my reflections whenever I have to
think about corporate racial blame for anything. He too has
a simple explanation for the white man's otherwise inex-
plicable behavior: *"By nature* they are devils! *By nature* they
are incapable of loving you!"* Perhaps so. So easy a solution
is tempting in a world of complex motivations and conflicting values. But if I accept Muhammad's premise, I have to
start wondering *what I am* "by nature," and whether the
white man and I are essentially any different.

I have a friend, a professional man of exceptional education, whose bitterness is so deep that when he sees white
children on the street, he invariably utters an oath. Of if there
is a touching story on the television or in the news involving
a white child he will turn the television off or put the newspaper away in disgust. His explanation is that "they present
those little bastards like gods and goddesses when they're
kids; and yet you know that when they grow up they'll be
sons-of-bitches just like their fathers, and they will make it
just as tough for your kid and mine as their parents have
made it for us!" On one occasion he admitted that if he had
his way, he would "strangle every little blue-eyed bastard"
he could catch. This man is not a Black Muslim. He is not a
black nationalist of any affiliation. Indeed, he is a respected
member of a respected church. Each time I see him I cannot
help seeing in my mind's eye his white counterpart, who
belongs to the "First Church" and the White Citizens Coun-

cil, and who believes firmly that "*all* niggers are dangerous and have to be kept in their places."

In the heart of the black racist there burns the fervent desire to "see the white man get what is coming to him." This I call the "Armageddon Complex," after the fervent longing in the heart of every Black Muslim to see that great day dawn when the final confrontation between good and evil, black men and white men, will take place. The Armageddon Complex is certainly not new. Throughout the long reaches of history it, or something very much like it, must have helped to sustain many a subject people when every other reason to continue to try to endure must have left them. The Negro's spirituals in large number reflect the desire to see his enemies humbled. The "nonviolent" students who have suffered so much at the hands of the non-nonviolent thugs who do not understand the meaning of nonviolence, still want to "overcome." With charity, one may assume that what they want to overcome is prejudice, not persons. Even to so sensitive and gifted a poet as Claude McKay, the thought of vengeance made death itself endurable:

> If we must die, let it not be like dogs
> Hunted and penned in some inglorious spot,
> While round us bark the mad and hungry dogs
> Making their mock at our accursed lot.
> If we must die, O let us nobly die,
> So that our precious blood may not be shed
> In vain; then even the monsters we defy
> Shall be constrained to honor us though dead!
> O kinsmen! We must meet the common foe!
> Though far out-numbered let us show us brave,
> And for their thousand blows deal one death blow!
> What though before us lies the open grave?

Like men we'll face the murderous, cowardly pack,
Pressed to the wall, dying but fighting back![3]

However tragic may be the prospect of armed revolution, or of at least some kind of a continuing racially inspired guerrilla warfare, the tenseness of the present situation in America permits no denial of the possibility. Armed white bands have carried out constant attacks against Negroes living and working in the South since 1954, and even before. Various kinds of "vigilante" groups dedicated to the maintenance of "the Southern way of life" have been responsible for an untold number of mutilations and murders in the state of Mississippi and elsewhere. Until two young white men working with CORE disappeared (along with a Negro coworker) near Philadelphia, Mississippi in June of 1964, neither the armed whites nor their behavior drew much attention from the press or from those charged with the maintenance of law and order. In Mississippi it was taken for granted. What is dangerous to all of us is that the rest of America takes *Mississippi* for granted, that it is a "closed society," and that anyone who goes there, particularly if he happens not to be white, does so at his own risk. Claude Sitton, Atlanta-based correspondent of the *New York Times*, writes with candor and restraint of the situation in Mississippi in the *Times* June 3:

> Many whites and Negroes are armed. The Ku Klux Klan and such vigilante groups as the Americans for the Preservation of the White Race have apparently won a substantial number of recruits. Sporadic anti-Negro terrorism has plagued some areas . . .
>
> There have been numerous reports of threats, harassment and intimidation against civil rights workers, Negroes and

newsmen. Some incidents have involved armed whites cruising the streets, highways and country roads after dark in automobiles from which the license plates have been removed . . . There is no evidence that the efforts of the Federal authorities to prevent interference with the voter registration drive have had much effect on the whites.

It is obvious that we already have in the South organized, armed bands which are permitted to operate under anonymity—automobiles without license plates, hoods, etc., and who are but little affected even by the federal presence. Perhaps the two most fundamental values available in this society are life itself and the right to vote (the means by which one maintains his freedom). When a national state cannot, or *will* not, guarantee the right to life and liberty in theory *and in fact*, it becomes increasingly vulnerable to destruction from within and from without.

Many New Yorkers are disturbed over the so-called Maccabees, a vigilante organization organized by the Hasidic Jews of Brooklyn. While it is claimed that the "Maccabees" have no racial axe to grind, but only the protection of their women, etc., one is reminded that the Ku Klux Klan sprang originally from the same noble sentiments. The Maccabees are said to be unarmed, but this makes them no less dangerous. The Black Muslims are not armed either, at least not yet. But arming is a simple (and logical) matter once an already organized group feels itself called upon to act. Doubtless the Hasidic Jews are understandably frustrated over the failure of the regularly constituted law enforcement agencies to enforce the law adequately for their protection and security. This is a frustration that Negroes are expected to accept as a normal way of life.

So far there has been no national alarm over the presence
or organized armed or unarmed whites in the country, but
the increased sense of alienation among Negroes and the
brooding, explosive presence of Malcolm X make the question of armed Negroes a matter of national concern, not
only because of the prospect of bloodshed, but because of
the implications of a resort to arms. A resort to arms would
mean among other things that the Negro's historic faith in
America and in the white man's justice had come finally to
an end. It would mean that the hope for an integrated society
is at an end, or that the belief in integration itself is no longer
attractive to "the critical mass" of Negroes who have themselves fought for it and led others to adopt its feasibility as
a desirable way of life. It would mean possibly that the
American Negro has at last turned outside his homeland for
help.

Many of the more liberal white and Negro civil rights
leaders have heretofore tacitly welcomed the presence of
Malcolm X as a kind of catalytic agent for the civil rights
movement. The theory has been that as long as Malcolm was
the leader of a "Third Force" which was obviously more
extreme than any integrationist organization, the segregationists would prefer some integration to an all-out race war.
But few civil rights leaders really thought that Malcolm was
prepared to do much other than talk, as long as he remained
subject to the strict discipline of Elijah Muhammad. Now
Malcolm is no longer subject to that discipline, and there is
an increasing apprehension that he may attempt "something
dramatic" which will seriously damage the integrationist
cause.

New tensions in Harlem have underscored this fear. In

April and May of 1964 New York police brought to light
the existence of a black terrorist organization of Harlem
Negro youth allegedly trained by Malcolm X or some of his
followers. The members of the organization, known as the
Blood Brothers, are well trained in Judo and karate, and have
been held responsible for the murder of at least four whites
in Harlem.

A casual survey of Harlem will startle the average New
Yorker with the evidence that intra-group gang fights among
Negroes have almost disappeared. There is a new interest,
even among the youth, in racial solidarity, and a correspond-
ing increase in out-group hostility. There is probably no
place in the Western Hemisphere more (black) nationalistic
than Harlem, and few anywhere. The Black Nationalists
under Malcolm's leadership are largely responsible for this.
Whether his influence will continue as leader of the Muslim
Mosque, Inc., it is much too early to say, but there is little
reason to believe that it will not.

James Wechsler of the *New York Post* quotes Malcolm
as describing his vision of Harlem as a firmly-ruled black
community in which "no white man will set foot without a
guide." "In his tortured dream," Wechsler said, "the black
populace—during this period of transition before the ultimate
return to Africa—will build Algerian-type walls around its
own sectors, and thus achieve at least temporary escape from
white persecution. One can only sadly observe that Georgia's Senator Richard Russell would probably find this a
satisfactory formula for the settlement of the race problem."

It would be a mistake to assume that such chauvinistic
sentiments are restricted to a few radicals like Malcolm X.
While the responsible Negro leaders are doing all they can

do, they cannot do enough. Theirs is a continual race against time, and they are constantly under attack from the impatient and the radical. Maurice Quami bespoke a growing mood of black impatience when he attacked Martin Luther King, Jr., for "having tea in the White House, and having titles conferred upon you which should come after you are free."[4] In lashing out at King, or Wilkins, or Farmer, the Negro "mass-man" is venting his frustration upon the symbols of his defeat. Negro leadership will never be able to deliver at a rate satisfactory to those they are attempting to lead to freedom. The forces of resistance have been too firmly entrenched too long. If America finds herself in real trouble, it will not be because Negro leadership has failed, but because America herself has failed. Norman Cousins, writing in the *Saturday Review*, reminds us that the problem derives from the condition of the Negro in America, and that the real incendiary centers are in the North—in the *black ghettos* of Chicago, Detroit and New York:

> New York's Harlem has all the volatile makings of one of the worst race riots in history. If it comes, the villains will not just be the black hotheads and know-nothings who incited people to riot. The villains will include all the whites who have abused, shunned, cheated, hounded, and outraged the Negro beyond endurance: the landlords who overcharge and whose tenements violate all the laws of housing safety; the housing inspectors who ignore the violations; the white merchants who short-weigh, short-change, and pass off inferior merchandise; education officials who are clearly incapable of meeting the incredibly difficult challenge of operating a school system in Harlem; white employers who may deplore racial injustice, but who have yet to institute decent employment practices in their own firms; union leaders who proclaim their interest in the

working man but who draw color lines as rigid as the most
segregated community; in short, everyone who thinks the
problem is at a distance.[5]

Mr. Cousins is right of course. The house of cards that
masquerades as "interracial goodwill" or "interracial under-
standing" South *or* North, is doomed to collapse. The question is not if, but when; not whether, but why. The question
is who will bring it about and whether for private ends or
for the public good. It is asking too much of history to expect that we may continue indefinitely as we have in the past.
We cannot and we must not. In St. Augustine and elsewhere,
the Negroes demonstrating in the streets have been joined
by counter-forces of white demonstrators, Klan elements
among them. There has been no protection for the Negroes
who have remained "nonviolent" in spite of the most intense
provocation. In Harlem, the situation is reversed. There it is
the whites who are set upon. But, the black nationalists argue,
the situations are not analogous, for in Harlem the white
man, while despising the Negro, comes into his community
to exploit and plunder him, and for no other reason. And so
the blacks are swarming and dreaming of a black casbah—a
self-imposed *black ghetto*, but protected from the forces
which created it in the first place. An interesting bit of
poetry illustrates the mood, the fulfillment, of the Armageddon Complex:

    i wonder where i will be when
    railroads run on c.p.t.* when
    malcolm x is prime minister
    of the nation of islam
    just outside san diego.

what will i do when banks close
on crispus attucks day?

will i be a black hipster
and swing with all the whites
because its the thing to do?
or a social worker going each day
into the W.A.S.P.** ghetto and coming out
proud that i have helped the masses?

will all whites look the same to me
will i speak to them as "you people"
will my maid, months past 53, still be a girl
to me?
or to save my skin (now preferred) will i say
to soothe the troubled folk who pin me to
the wall in debate, "it's not me, some of my best
friends are white!"
or will i be a *liberal*?

and sit with whites
because i'm black
and wear their friendship
as a beacon of rebellion
and pat myself on my back
because they are white and
i am black.

when the question of the day is:
"WOULD YOU LIKE YOUR SISTER TO MARRY A WHITE?"
and the masses sing "old white saul"
and a bust of lumumba stands in central park
and president martin luther king celebrates his
seventh term in office by playing golf with
poet laureate, langston hughes, on the black house lawn,
while the speaker of the house, james baldwin, sits
and the heavyweight champion of the world is white!
sipping gin,
where will i be?

i hope i can walk down the street as though nothing
has happened, because
this too will pass.[6]

We may sit on our hands and hope that the problem
will go away. We may, if we choose, continue to dole out
little bits of democracy like bribes to a peevish, insistent
child. We may discount Malcolm X as the symbol of anything except a personal lust for power. And we may, if it
pleases us, ignore the stirrings in the *black ghetto* that look
toward some kind of Armageddon, soon or late. We may
revel in our social somnambulism until some rude awakening
—when it will very likely be too late to do then what we
should be doing now. But we will pay a horrible and un-
necessary price, and we will be lucky if it need not be paid
in blood.

Malcolm X is not alone in his belief that a racial con-
flagration in this country and perhaps on a global scale is the
shortest and surest solution to the problems of this civilization. The primacy of the white races of the West over the
past five hundred years did not win friends for them, and
hatred for the white man is not confined to the *black ghettos*
of America. This is the price of conquest, and all conquering
peoples have paid it. But the point to be established here is
that the Negro in America, who has received less consideration and more abuse from the hands of the American white
man than any other people anywhere in the world, has
stood steadfastly behind him (and, when permitted, beside
him), with a degree of patience and loyalty that is unique in
the annals of time. Let the white man recognize this now,
before it is too late, and learn to love mercy and do justly.

The old order of things has in truth passed away. The old values and taboos that meant so much before are worthless in today's world, or will be soon. Never mind the color of a man's skin. That is the least important index of his worth. If Malcolm X means anything, it is that America has but a little time to learn the meaning of color, which is, that it has no meaning.

Notes

CHAPTER 1

1. From *Poems in Protest*, an unpublished manuscript by C. Eric Lincoln.

2. Quoted in Gunnar Myrdal's *American Dilemma* (New York: Harper and Row, Publishers, 1944), Vol. I, p. 4.

3. Charles Silberman, *Crisis in Black and White* (New York: Random House, Inc., 1964), p. 10.

4. *See* C. Eric Lincoln, *The Black Muslims in America* (Boston: Beacon Press, 1961).

5. John Steinbeck, *New York Amsterdam News*, July 30, 1960. Reprinted from *The Saturday Review*.

6. The Reverend A. Powell Davies, former pastor, All Souls Unitarian Church, Washington, D.C.

7. James Baldwin, "A Letter to My Nephew," *The Progressive*, December, 1962.

8. Quoted in part from C. Eric Lincoln, "The Legacy of Freedom," *The Averill Lecture*, delivered at Colby College, Winter, 1962.

9. John Hope Franklin, "Civil Rights in American History," *The Progressive*, December, 1962.

10. Joseph R. Washington, Jr., *Black Religion* (Boston: Beacon Press, 1964).

11. From the sonnet by Emma Lazarus on a tablet inside the main entrance to the Statue of Liberty.

12. Benjamin Brawley, "The Negro in Spanish Exploration," *A Social History of the American Negro* (New York: The Macmillan Company, 1921).

13. The First Chinese Exclusion Act was passed in 1882.

14. The Immigration Quota Law of 1924 limited the annual number of immigrants to 2 percent of each country's representation in the United States in 1880. After 1927, the total number admitted could not exceed 150,000 annually. The law did not apply to European nations.

15. Walter Rauschenbusch, *Christianizing the Social Order* (New York: The Macmillan Company, 1926).

16. Martin Luther King, *Why We Can't Wait* (New York: Harper and Row, Publishers, 1964).

17. *The Atlanta Constitution*, April 26, 1964.

18. "No man is born a personality; everyone has first to make himself into a personality by obedience towards another instinct, which leads to unity and homogeneity." Ernst Troeltsch, *Christian Thought* (New York: Meridian Books, 1957), p. 77. Cf. Walter G. Muelder, *Foundations of the Responsible Society* (New York: Abingdon Press, 1959), p. 24.

19. Arnold J. Toynbee, *A Study of History* (2nd ed., London: Oxford University Press, 1935), Vol. I, p. 224.

20. Thomas Pettigrew, "The Myth of the Moderates," *The Christian Century*, May 24, 1961.

21. Benjamin Mays in *The Christian Century,* April 22, 1964.

22. "The Myth of the Moderates," *op. cit.*

CHAPTER 2

1. Lincoln, *Poems in Protest, op. cit.*

2. Adapted from C. Eric Lincoln, "The Legacy of Freedom," *Perspective—The Colby Alumnus*, Winter, 1962.

3. Arna Bontemps, *Story of the Negro* (New York: Alfred A. Knopf, Inc., 1958).

4. Herbert Aptheker, in his work *American Negro Slave Revolts*, lists 250 revolts and conspiracies as having occurred in the continental United States.

5. *See* Lerone Bennett, *Before the Mayflower* (Chicago: Johnson Publishing Co., 1962).

6. *Ibid.*

7. Bontemps, *op. cit.*

8. Quoted in E. Franklin Frazier, *The Negro in the United States* (New York: The Macmillan Company, 1949).

9. Bennett, *op. cit.*

10. *Ibid.*

11. *Ibid.*

12. *Ibid.*

13. Franklin, *op. cit.*

14. Langston Hughes, *Fight for Freedom* (New York: Berkley Publishing Corporation, 1962).

15. *See* C. Eric Lincoln, "The Black Muslims as a Protest Movement," *Assuring Freedom to the Free*, ed. Arnold Rose (Detroit: Wayne University Press, 1963).

16. Hughes, *op. cit.*

17. *Ibid.*

18. *U.S. News and World Report*, Feb. 29, 1964.

19. *Ibid.*

20. *Ibid.*

21. For a discussion of protest as a means of communication, *see* C. Eric Lincoln, "Patterns of Protest: Slavery and Freedom," *The Christian Century*, June 3, 1964, from which part of the present discussion was taken.

CHAPTER 3

1. Lincoln, *Poems in Protest, op. cit.*

2. W. E. B. Du Bois, *Black Folk Then and Now* (New York: Holt, Rinehart & Winston, Inc., 1939).

3. Bertram P. Karon, *The Negro Personality* (New York: Springer Publishing Co., Inc., 1958).

4. Abram Kardiner and Lionel Ovesey, *The Mark of Oppression* (New York: W. W. Norton & Company, Inc., 1951), pp. 325-326.

5. Harold Isaacs, *The American Negro and Africa: Some Notes.* Read before the Second Annual Conference, The American Society of African Culture. New York, June 28, 1959.

6. Daniel Bell, "Plea for a 'New Phase in Negro Leadership,'" *The New York Times*, May 31, 1964.

7. Edmund David Cronon, *Black Moses* (Madison: The University of Wisconsin Press, 1955), p. 47.

8. Harold Isaacs, *The New World of Negro Americans* (New York: The John Day Co., 1963).

9. *See* C. Eric Lincoln, "The Black Muslims and Christian Conscience," *Concern*, Sept 5, 1963.

10. *See* C. Eric Lincoln, *The Black Muslims in America, op. cit.*

11. "A Conversation with James Baldwin," *Freedomways*, Summer, 1963.

12. *See Freedomways*, Fall, 1961, and Summer, 1963.

CHAPTER 4

1. Lincoln, *Poems in Protest*, op. cit.

2. This vignette on a visit with Muhammad was originally written for the *Negro Digest* and appeared under the title "A Visit With Muhammad," April, 1964.

3. C. Eric Lincoln, "Extremist Attitudes in the Black Muslim Movement," *The Journal of Social Issues*, April, 1963. *See also* by the same author, "Black Muslims—Mirror of the Existing Order," *New South*, January, 1963.

4. The foregoing excerpts in this series are all from the text of a prepared news release given out by Malcolm X at his news conference at the Park Sheraton Hotel, New York City, on March 12, 1964.

5. *See The Black Muslims in America, op. cit.*

6. Milton Galamison, *The Liberator*, May, 1963.

7. John Morsell, *The Crisis*, April, 1964.

8. *Ibid.*

9. Quoted by James Wechsler, "The Cult of Malcolm X," *The Progressive*, June, 1964.

CHAPTER 5

1. Lincoln, *Poems in Protest, op. cit.*

2. James Weschler, *The Progressive*, June, 1964.

3. Quoted in John Hope Franklin, *From Slavery to Freedom* (New York: Alfred A. Knopf, Inc., 1956).

4. Martin Quami, *The Liberator*, May, 1963.

5. Norman Cousins, *The Saturday Review*, May 30, 1964.

6. This poem was received from an anonymous writer. It allegedly was published by "JB," under the title "Nate and Rosey, Es Salam Alaikum," *Stylus*, Vol. 6, No. 2, Spring, 1962, Temple University, Philadelphia. I cannot vouch for the original.